COMMUNICATIONS
— & —
RELATIONSHIPS

Also by the Author:

What my clients taught me about taking better care of myself!
... the little blue book that opened my and many others' eyes to the potential of "Wellness", and it changed our lives!

Finding Balance
... to the many persons in education and the other helping professions I have had the privilege of serving during my 50-year career.

COMMUNICATIONS
&
RELATIONSHIPS

DAN ROSIN, Ph.D.

Copyright © 2023 Dan Rosin, Ph.D.

All rights reserved. No part of this book may be reproduced, stored, or transmitted by any means—whether auditory, graphic, mechanical, or electronic—without written permission of both publisher and author, except in the case of brief excerpts used in critical articles and reviews. Unauthorized reproduction of any part of this work is illegal and is punishable by law.

ISBN: 979-8-88640-609-2 (sc)
ISBN: 979-8-88640-610-8 (hc)
ISBN: 979-8-88640-611-5 (e)

Because of the dynamic nature of the Internet, any web addresses or links contained in this book may have changed since publication and may no longer be valid. The views expressed in this work are solely those of the author and do not necessarily reflect the views of the publisher, and the publisher hereby disclaims any responsibility for them.

One Galleria Blvd., Suite 1900, Metairie, LA 70001
1-888-421-2397

*I dedicate this book to all those people who worked
so hard to make a better life for themselves and their partner.*

ACKNOWLEDGEMENTS

I would like to thank the following people who have provided me the opportunity to fulfill my dreams.

My wife Drinda, whose support in all aspects of my life has allowed me to reach for "my stars".

Our children Lisa and Brad, who have always been my inspiration and who have always kept me grounded in reality.

My mother Emerald, who truly believed I could "do anything". Nancy and Jay Easterbrook, who have provided me with the solitude and affordable housing (Cayman Island) in which to write both my books.

My friends and technicians—Jay Easterbrook (photographer), Jenny Gates (editor), Brian Hydesmith (designer), Pascal Pernix (photographer), and Josh Watt (reader).

To you all, my deepest gratitude.

CONTENTS

Introduction xiii

Relationships

Differences 1
Appreciated, But Not Equal 3
The Language of #1 4
Friendship 6
Spark 8
Lust Just Doesn't Cut It 10
Language of Love 12
Good Buttons—Bad Buttons 14
Red Flag Theory 16
Sitting in the Mud 18
After the Affair 20
Penance 22
People vs. Accomplishment 23
Let's Make It Official 25
"Giving In" Isn't the Answer 27
You're Smothering Me! 29
Tasks vs. People 31
I Meet You and Then I Give Up My Friends? 34
"Nothing or All" Principle 37
Blinded by the Vision 39
Backyard (cont.) 40
Dysfunctional Family Fallout 42
Stop the Hurt and Move On! 44
"He's Back With the Red Head" 46
Fulfillment 48
She's a Keeper 49

Communication

- 93% of Communication … 51
- "You" Language 53
- The Other Person's Truth 55
- Men and Women are Different, so Let's Stop Making Such a Big Deal of it!... 57
- Don't Fight—Express!... 59
- Don't Go for the Win—Discuss 60
- All Perspectives are Equal, but Mine is More Equal 63
- Confrontation and Its Relationship to Winning............................ 65
- So What Would I Have to Do? 67
- Discussion/Conversation: The Building Blocks of Communication 68
- Want To Be Successful Socially? Learn To Listen!....................... 70
- "Not Accepted" is Preferable to "Being Rejected" 72
- You Have to Listen if You are Going to Hear Anything! 74
- Stoppers—Anger and Hurt.. 76
- Maybe It's Okay to be a Little Crazy?.. 78
- Talk to Me! 81

Change

- Successful Change Requires Consciousness, Focus and Repetition ... 83
- You Need to Feel Safe to Change 84
- Change is About Options 86
- We are Both Doing Good Work! 87
- The Best Predictor… 89
- That's a Choice, Not a Condition 91

Personal Power

- Understandable, but No Longer Appropriate 92
- To My Parents.. 94
- Homework for a Victim 95

Self-Esteem

- Ego 96
- Needy! 97

Light Your Lamp 98
Update and Upgrade! 100
Four Paths of Low Self-Esteem 102
Watch Your Language... 103
Write, Share, Bury and Burn! 105

Strokes

Stroke Pot 107
External and Internal Strokes 109
Strokes and Statespersons 111
Strokes as a Mathematical Formula 113
Me First 115
React or Respond? 117
Need or Want? 119
Antibodies and Immunity 121
Strokes From Self—Who Would Have Thought?! 122
Humble Gone Bad 124
Muddied Waters 126
Stingy With Strokes 127

Beliefs

Beliefs Drive Behaviour 129
Irrational Feelings and Beliefs 130
Filter 134
Good Guilt 135
Clean Slate 137
Guilt—A Teaching Tool 139

Anger

Anger and Assumptions 141
Righteous Anger and the QL Meter 143
More Than Discipline 146
Anger 148

Assertiveness

Expectations or Assertiveness 150

Finding Your Voice 153
Mothers Have Rights! 155

Other

Why Questions? 157
Why + Worry = No Action 159
I Don't Need You to be Different for Me to be Okay! 160
Stress and Serotonin 162
Which Hook? 164
It's Just a TV Show 166
Don't Trust, Don't Share, and Don't Get Close! 167
How Many Chances Should I Give You? 168
New Big Three 170
Treating "Panic Attacks" 171
Preaching 173
In Control 176
Decision Making 177
The Value of Acquaintances 178
Say "Yes" to Yourself 180
Abandonment Issues 181
The Adult (A) of a Child of an Alcoholic 183
What a Character! 185
The Contract 187
Weight Filter 188
Invite People to Think, Not to Fight! 190
Therapist—Magician or Cheerleader? 192
Wellness, Despite the Early Messages 193
Love Begins With Respect 194
Regret! 195
Stability! 197
Significant Moments 199
The Fourth Primary Influencer 201
Time Together Isn't the Whole Answer, but 203
Defining Moment 206
Two Streams of Learning 209

INTRODUCTION

I am not sure why I chose to write in the style I have—short, concise, one- to three-page concepts. These concepts express my ideas, thoughts and insights in a succinct manner, and perhaps this writing style is indicative of how I think and learn best myself. Give me a germ of an idea and I'll think it through, flush it out, embellish it (at times), and make it fit my logical way of seeing the world.

When reading this book, I ask you to work at forming your own interpretations of the concepts, not just accept what I think I learned. A suggestion from a colleague in using this book is to have both partners read the same concept and then discuss it together. Two beneficial things occur—they learn something new, and are encouraged to communicate on things that might assist their relationship to reach a new level of openness and honesty.

Communication and Relationships was written in the same style as my first book "Finding Balance". One of the things that makes it so easy to read and understand is that in using the "concept" form of writing, the reader doesn't have to plough through pages and pages, or an entire chapter, to get to the "meat and potatoes" of what is being said. It's all there on one or two pages.

In my work, people enter into therapy hoping to make their lives better, and it is my job to assist them to get their needs met. In addition to helping them, I also get something out of it. During the therapeutic process I often feel the atmosphere get highly energized and my creative juices get seriously piqued. It has thus been at this moment of infused creative energy that the majority of concepts were conceptualized and eventually found their way into this book.

With my previous book ***Finding Balance*** it was suggested by a major book publisher that I convert the concept method of presenting the material to a tips method— "100 Tips On How To Have A Better Life". It is ironic that after submitting my manuscript to several publishers, the only one to respond suggests that I totally change the book to a tips book. It's funny now, but at the time, I was totally indignant and responding with somewhat of a martyr's attitude: "I would rather maintain the integrity of this book as it was written than sell (out) a thousand tip books." Interesting stance; however, I still feel the same today.

Rather than ***Communication & Relationships*** being filled with tips, it presents "new ways of working with real issues", methods I created while I was engaged in the therapeutic process. It is the creative "Ah, ahs" that came about in therapy that are the essence of the concepts in this book.

Communication & Relationships is about real people with real problems. It was written from many experiences that took place while couples were in therapy with me. The cases described are actual composites of many different sessions with many different clients. The book is written for people who seek understanding of the problems they face in their everyday lives. By reading these stories/concepts about people just like them, and seeing how they and the therapist dealt with the problem, they can learn how to better deal with their own issues.

DIFFERENCES

Men and women are different! It doesn't matter what these *differences* are based on—gender or personality—or where they come from. What does matter is that we recognise that men and women often have differing views on most issues.

Couples need exceptional communication skills to move past the differences between them. Unfortunately, few people possess these skills, and even fewer understand the need for them.

I believe that in order to successfully function as a "unit", individuals must come to accept each other's perceptions and acknowledge that it is okay to see things differently. As well, we need to recognise that those *differences are strengths*. It is important that each individual in a successful couple respect both their own position and that of their partner.

By contrast, some inappropriate responses to your partner's difference of opinion or perception would be to argue that either "You accept my perception as the correct one or you are not acceptable to me", or "I will work at changing you, to have you see and accept the 'best' way, which happens to be how I see things!" These arrogant responses put a great deal of pressure on a relationship. They reflect an attitude that says I have the *Universal Truth*.[1] The relationship then becomes about power, where whoever is louder and longer or colder and more sullen wins.

---

[1] Dan Rosin, *Finding Balance,* The Ewings Publishing, 2022, p. 84

However, there should be no "winner or loser" in a relationship because then we have two losers. Therefore, it is of prime importance that we accept our partner's differences and realize that they are not out to get us. Rather, that our partner possesses a treasure trove of fundamental values and beliefs that need to be respected and worked with, not changed.

Everybody is different, and that's okay!

APPRECIATED, BUT NOT EQUAL

Like the actor in a play with only a few lines, the entire production positively benefits when those few lines are spoken correctly and at exactly the right time. However, if you screw those lines up, you are no longer trusted to perform your role and the entire production suffers. If one person in a relationship is very competent, extremely efficient, and even controlling—or the exact opposite—there is often no problem between them unless the other partner is made to feel invaluable, or that what they do bring to the relationship is not appreciated.

Like the actor's lines in a play, it's not always the amount you contribute when in the relationship, but how well it fits together at the end of the day, at the finale of the production. Some partners are social, others are not. Some need to be in the limelight, others would die if they were thrust onto centre stage. Some cook, others eat!

As long as both partners feel they are appreciated for their contribution to the relationship, then these individual differences do not have to be a factor or cause the relationship to fail.

> **It's not necessarily how much
> you contribute to a relationship.
> It's how much you're appreciated
> for what you do contribute.
> And don't forget that "timing" is everything!**

THE LANGUAGE OF #1

Rule #1 (2, 3, 4, etc.) – Make Your Partner #1 In Your Life!

He was the stereotypical male! The only time I ever saw him was when he got kicked out of the bedroom, and then he would come for only a session or two until "she came to her senses". Hmm!

He had a problem and it was "her attitude". As of late, she had made it clear that she was not interested in his "routine sex" demands, which were every other night. He was baffled and angry. Name calling wasn't enough; he brought out the Bible and preached to her. Apparently, having sex with him was her "God directed duty". And yes, he was serious!

He shared a number of frosty conversations that he and his wife had had recently. My feelings were that unless he learned the *"Language of #1"*, the ice-covered wall that seemed to be growing between them would only get thicker and higher.

The *Language of #1* is the language you can use to invite your partner to feel that they are the most important person in your life. It means consistently doing what your partner would recognize as loving and respectful behaviours. It means using your words and actions in ways that say, "You really matter to me". This means accepting your partner's "no", as in "no sex tonight", as an act of love on your part and not an act of rejection from them.

I shared the concept of *passionate yes, courageous no,* which is about having the courage and giving ourselves permission to say "no" to others so that we will have the energy and passion to say "yes" when we choose to be involved.[2]

---

[2] Dan Rosin, *Communication & Relationships,* The Ewings Publishing, 2023, p. 180.

A light bulb went on. He began to understand that getting what he wanted from his wife and, for that matter, his children and colleagues, depended a great deal on how he responded to their wants and needs. Not just his own.

Hey, this is not brain surgery!

Making your partner #1 in your life is insurance— for a vastly improved relationship.

FRIENDSHIP

Either they argued loudly and often, or didn't speak to each other for weeks at a time.

Since day one of their relationship, her biggest complaint was, "He's always out with the boys." While he had many male friends upon whom he depended for his social life—fishing, pool, going to hockey, baseball games, drinking beer into the early morning—his wife of 21 years was not included. Twenty-one years of marriage and, according to her, his newest "best friend" was a neighbour he'd only recently met.

The person who replaced her and with whom he spent most of his time just happened to own an antique automobile and a small refrigerator in his garage. She explained to me that in the past, she had tried everything to get his attention. But now even her tears and angry out-bursts were falling on deaf ears. She was becoming desperate.

I made the comment, "It sounds to me like you and your husband are not very friendly, and are not good friends. That he sees 'the boys' as being his friends and not you."

"You think?" was her sarcastic response. "We're not even close to being friends." Her response prompted me to do some serious thinking about the role of friendship in the context of an intimate relationship, and my response to her was:

> *When we first start a relationship with someone, we often want to be with and do everything with them. In time, this can change as a result of the pressures of work, children, aging parents, health issues, and the "power dynamics" that evolve between individuals who live together. Change is good, healthy and inevitable. But when one partner changes so much that they go from being your "best friend" to your "chief antagonist", then the relationship experiences much distress.*

That's what had happened to this woman and her husband. They had become "worst friends".

Her curiosity was heightened when I suggested to her that "Someone has to break the deadlock you've found yourselves in. And it might as well be you." In fact, it *had* to be her because he refused to attend.

The challenge I suggested was that she be her husband's *best friend* for the next several weeks and monitor whatever changes occurred. She thought about it, shrugged her shoulders, smiled wryly, and said, "Sure." Then, at some point in the future, after he had an opportunity to experience her change in behaviour, she was to talk with him about the concept of friendship in their relationship and how this might lead to them treating each other much better than they were.

All too often, partners *talk* about what they need to do to make things better. But they either never get around to making the changes—procrastination—or they become so annoyed at their partner's perceived "lack of trying", that they give up and revert back to old behaviours.

She agreed to say nothing about what she was doing for several weeks—being his best friend—and then to ask him if he was aware of any changes in her behaviour. When she felt that enough time had passed and her behaviour *was* noticeable to him, she was to ask him if he liked and appreciated these changes. She was to then engage him in a conversation about the importance of friendship in a relationship. This was a plan based on "change first and talk about it later".

If you are considering implementing the "best friend" practice to your own relationship, I would suggest that you think very seriously about two questions—do you really want this person for a friend, and do you really want to be friendly to this person?

Don't react too quickly or get too glib with the "Of course; they're my partner" response. Being a friend is hard work, time consuming, and you have to sacrifice. If you're going to put the energy into working at this relationship and at least one of you hasn't for quite awhile, then let's be really sure we care for this person and that we want them to care about us.

Do you really want this person to be friendly toward you?
Do you really want to put the energy into
being a friend to this person?
Be careful what you agree to!

SPARK

"We don't have a proper relationship. We are like brother and sister, or two friends who live together. We don't fight but we don't make love either."

Yes, they needed to work on their communication, on spending time together. Yes, they needed to stop letting the world get their best time and energy. Yes, they needed to relearn to play as individuals and then as a couple.

But one of their greatest obstacles to achieving these goals was their belief that the solution lay outside of themselves. They were looking for a quick fix to their lacklustre, passionless relationship, and they chose me! That belief netted them the following response:

> *It's not enough to live together, plan fun activities together, and have a joint bank account. You have to genuinely work at a relationship. Remember when you could hardly wait to see your partner and couldn't keep your hands off each other? Well, that's spark.*
>
> *Spark is the feeling that exists between two people that makes their relationship so special. It's more than a sexual feeling; it's based on respect, trust and mutual caring.*
>
> *I once believed that spark was either there or it wasn't. That it just happened, and once it was gone, there wasn't much you could do about it. I saw people who wanted their partner to be responsible for their spark. I believed that if two people treated each other a certain way, or if they stopped doing things that the other person didn't like, then they would feel that spark again for each other. In other words, I believed that one person's ability to feel that spark for their significant*

other was based on their significant other's behaviour toward them. It is a factor!

However, having observed a multitude of relationships over the years, I now see this very differently! The spark in a relationship can indeed be rekindled, but not from what you do or don't do for me, rather from what I do for you. Yes, my feelings for you will change more rapidly and have a more significant impact when I do the majority of the work.

If I am the person who feels the least amount of spark— who most wants "out" of the relationship—and I choose to work hard at our relationship and do those things that would tell you I care about you, then it is me who will benefit the most and who will feel the most change in relation to the spark between us.

Couples often want a quick fix when they feel that they have lost their "spark" for one another. And when this quick fix solution is not forthcoming the way they thought that it would be, then they often have a tendency to adopt a "forget it" attitude. For someone who doesn't have much "caring" left in them and where the spark has seemingly been snuffed out, it is easier to understand the notion that the "fix" or the "solution" lies within their partner than it is to get motivated to actually do something about it themselves.

I believe it is possible with focused caring and hard work couples can rekindle the spark in their relationship.

However they needed reminding that:

The amount of spark in a relationship is directly proportionate to the amount of work done on behalf of the relationship by both participants.

However, whoever has the least amount of feeling—spark—needs to work the hardest!

LUST JUST DOESN'T CUT IT

There they were, twenty-one years after they first met, sitting in my office wondering what went wrong. They had long ago stopped practising any kind of loving or caring behaviours toward each other. They were unhappy and frustrated.

They readily admitted that in their courting years, they had bypassed the caring, hand-holding, cuddling behaviours in favour of the more exciting forbidden fruit. They had never really practised being *respectful* or *courteous* to each other. Soon, the kids were born and life moved along. As they talked about their past together, they realized they had been "in lust", not in love. The question became, "Could two people who had not been particularly in love, but had been sexually attracted to each other, now find the formula to fall in love 21 years later, with the added difficulty of a couple of teenagers running around the house?"

Our challenge was to find the spark that had gone out of their relationship, if it was ever there. They needed to feel a spark, a desire for each other, or they were finished as a couple. In my view, the fact that they were in my office looking for help left me feeling hopeful.

Relationships can be restarted if one person is truly committed to working at it and, almost by sheer will, bring the other person along. Of course, it is much easier and more often successful if both persons are willing to work at the relationship. Working at the relationship is the key.

**Lust is like a Roman candle—
booming, bright and full of fizzle.**

"I didn't marry you because you were perfect. I didn't even marry you because I love you. I married you because you gave me a promise. That promise made up for your faults. And the promise I gave you made up for mine. Two imperfect people got married and it was the promise that made the marriage. And when our children were growing up, it wasn't a house that protected them and it wasn't our love that protected them — it was that promise."

—Thornton Wilder

LANGUAGE OF LOVE

I tell couples they need to speak the same *"Love Language"* as their partner if they are going to have a successful relationship.

In the course of our sessions, his wife identified what, in her mind, would be a reasonable standard by which she could identify that he still loved her—and this centred on the degree to which he supported her in bringing up the children. If he would do things with the children—and not because she wanted him to, but because he wanted to—then she could rest easy knowing that he still loved her.

In response to this revelation, all he could say was, "Huh!" in a disbelieving voice.

So she reiterated for him. If he would become more available and more patient with the kids, then she would feel more loved. She needed to know the kids were safe and cared for when they were in his charge. For her, this would validate her belief that she had "chosen the right person". Speaking her *language* also meant supporting her at her job. To do this, all he had to do was his fair share around the house.

By contrast, he thought that the right *language of love* meant having sex every other night, cutting the grass occasionally, and sacrificing by cutting his "extracurricular" time down to only one night a week out with the boys. A somewhat typical male, he was projecting his "language" onto hers. In actual fact, he missed "the language thing" by a mile!

He thought that loving her meant that he was supposed to say, "You're sexy and I am so excited about you being in my life." She thought that loving her meant he would say, "Let me help you get the kids to bed"—and not have to remind him to do so.

When they understood the meaning of the phrase *language of love* and how that language had changed over the years, particularly after the kids were born, the communication between them began to improve. It was not ideal, but it was getting better.

They both realized that they needed to discover what was important to their partner. Speaking the language of self-centredness was not conducive to conjugal cooperation and did not serve to meet either partner's needs in their relationship.

I have observed that this *"language of love"* concept fails miserably when either or both partners are lazy about staying conscious about their responsibility to their partners' needs, or they develop an attitude that says, "My needs are more important than yours."

Things will definitely fall apart in the relationship if there is no desire to do what is best for one's partner.

> **You don't need to understand "why"
> it's important to your partner. You only need
> to understand "what" they need and, within reason,
> to make an effort to make that happen.**

GOOD BUTTONS—BAD BUTTONS

Good Buttons are sensitivities that when reminded of, the person chooses behaviours that are consistent with the **Mechanics** and **Spirit** of a Good Relationship.

Bad Buttons are sensitivities that when reminded of, the person chooses behaviours that **Discount** others, constantly points out flaws and weaknesses, and invites anger.

Mechanics of a Good Relationship
- good Active Listener
- uses "I" language
- understands that nobody can change another person, but everybody has the right to express themselves (thoughts, feelings, values, beliefs)
- the goal is to be heard and to hear one's partner, not to change that partner
- practises appropriate behaviour

Spirit of a Good Relationship
- has a genuine interest in the partner's needs and wants, and has the desire to please
- maintains a positive attitude about most things
- works from the premise that their glass is half full, are positive, understands that negative people wear others out
- wants the relationship to be successful and is willing to work at it

I am smiling as I write this concept. I can hear the difference in my voice as I say *Goood Button—Baad Button.* Very few couples come to my office to share with me that their partner is constantly choosing to push their *good button*—is a good listener, courteous, and respectful. No! They come because their partner, consciously or otherwise, is leaning all over the *bad button* and they want it to stop.

They come asking how to stop pushing each other's bad buttons. I believe they should be asking, "How do we focus on pushing each other's good buttons" more often. Remember:

**What you start doing is far more significant
than what you stop doing!
Focus on each other's Good Buttons
rather than the Bad.**

RED FLAG THEORY

A message came to me late in the day to call a past client who wanted to start therapy again. We had spent several sessions the previous year examining her life. In particular, we looked at the choices she made regarding the men she invited into her life. Our sessions had suddenly stopped when she declared she had finally found "someone who really cares about me, my soul mate".

Her wanting to resume therapy probably meant it didn't work out. She was likely back to beating herself up for choosing poorly. She had probably resurrected the cycle that there was something wrong with her because she kept choosing men who used, abused and disregarded her.

When we met, she was very depressed. She realized that yet another relationship had failed and her self-esteem was at an all-time low. "Why do I always choose the wrong guys?" was her lament throughout our first session. "If I would only choose better …." I stopped her in mid-sentence and suggested to her that it wasn't about her needing to choose better. After all, who can do that well at the beginning of a relationship?

Instead, I suggested that the problem was probably more about her not acting on the *"red flags"* that the men presented. She chose to ignore the signals or to make excuses when they treated her poorly. She chose to keep them around, hoping they would change for the better. People in a new relationship present well. It is not possible in the beginnings of a relationship to see the real person; anyone can get snowed. So, should we stop looking for love in case they aren't who we think they are? I think not!

I encourage people to think positively and give the new relationship a fair chance. Forget about all those "what ifs", fears and worries borne from the past—easy to say—and stay open to the possibility that this relationship will work out. Do not focus on how you *might* get taken advantage of again.

Love the person and expect love back. If you don't feel that your feelings are reciprocated, talk to your partner. Lay it out confidently.

Keep giving feedback. Then, and only then, if things don't change, end it! Do the best you can. Work at the relationship. But do not become so emotionally tied-up in it that you are willing to accept abuse. Remember the old adage, "You can't make a silk purse out of a sow's ear."

No test exists for choosing the right person before you get to know them. If you are the kind of person who feels it is your duty to help others overcome themselves and their behaviours, stop it! And stop giving yourself hell for not trying to save all the defective relationships you may or have entered. It is not your job alone to save a relationship or make it work. In the future, be open to love. But when the Red Flags present themselves, act on them! Don't procrastinate! Jump all over those dubious behaviours with a thousand questions. And if you don't hear the right explanations, hit the eject button pronto.

If the "red flag" behaviours don't change—get out!

SITTING IN THE MUD

The "passage of time" is not the only way to get over a failed relationship. Sometimes, we have to work extra hard at saying goodbye.

I can recall the case of one of a person who took 12 years to get over his last relationship. In the meantime, he had remarried, but still clung to that original relationship. He would think about her and wonder how she was doing, even though she had treated him rather terribly.

Now here he was, three months after the disintegration of his most recent five-year marriage, feeling depressed, despondent, and very angry at his ex-wife's cavalier attitude. She had so coldly and matter-of-factly stated, "I want out, I'm done, and I have nothing further to say!" He didn't understand what he perceived to be a complete turnaround, and was still stuck months later. I likened it to "sitting in the mud".

I suggested his being stuck might be a result of the fact that he was still clinging to the possibility of reconciliation with his wife. He denied that. "I wouldn't have her back for all the … and besides, she is in another relationship and even had been before our relationship ended." He later recanted and stated that he would have her back in a second, despite the poor treatment he had received from her.

This concept of *sitting in the mud* arises from behaviours that are often a consequence of *poor self-esteem*. He had developed poor self-esteem earlier in his life and was quite willing to take back his partner and continue a toxic relationship. Sometimes we settle for what we think we are worth!

My question to him was, do we wait for the pain and anger to stop, or do we work at helping it go away? Since in his mind moving on was taking a very long time, he was quite open to "doing the work, saying goodbye and taking back his power". This time around, he did not wish to let the "interval of time" be his only tool to heal.

I suggested he write a *therapeutic letter*[3] to speed up the process of saying goodbye. She had physically left him, but he had not emotionally

---

[3] Rosin, *Finding Balance,* p. 78.

gotten over her and he needed to end it. He needed to give up his role of being the "dumped" victim. Letter writing would allow him one last "go-around" to express what was good and bad about the relationship, and what "could have been" if they had stayed together.

The process is: you write about the good, the bad and what "could have been" in the relationship. Then discuss what you wrote with your priest, minister or counsellor, and in this way let go of that person.

> **Getting over a failed relationship does not occur at the flip of a light switch. It's a process. Although it can't be rushed, it can be speeded up if we work at it!**

AFTER THE AFFAIR

You don't get past an affair, you work through it!

My client was having a very difficult time with the fact that her significant other had had an affair. A "one-night stand" that happened sometime in the *spring*. She felt betrayed and, contrary to his preference, thought it was far too soon to just "drop it and move on". There was more penance that remained to be served before she could put the issue behind her.

They talked a lot about the issue. He was a good listener, analyzed his own behaviour, admitted to his flaws and faults, was concerned about her, and appeared truly apologetic for his "mistake in judgement".

It was now *summer* and they felt stuck. They were past the shock, the hurt, and the decision of whether they should stay together, but they "weren't moving ahead". He admitted that he was beginning to "stop trying, because it didn't seem to make a difference". Sex was still "verboten", and even though he understood her resentment, he was beginning to tire of the punishment for a crime that, in his eyes, was "ancient history".

The balance point between her "I am still hurting" and his "Get over it and let's move on" was very tricky. He needed to respect her feelings and give her time to resolve the huge "loss of trust" that resulted from the affair. She needed to understand that if the issue were to go unresolved for too long, he would lose hope and could walk away from the relationship completely.

On her part, she was still trying her best to "get past it". On his part, he was doing his best to show understanding by giving her the time she needed. Everybody was doing their best, but they were still stuck.

Both of them used the term "get past it" several times. I wondered if a big part of their being stuck was a result of putting all positive behaviours on hold in their relationship until they both "got past it".

I suggested that waiting to "get past it" was not the most proactive approach that either of them could do under the circumstances. After all, they both wanted to move on, and perhaps this path of passive waiting for feelings to change would not work. They decided to take some action.

He took it upon himself to learn new, pleasing behaviours and worked on new communication skills. She agreed to stop focusing on "getting past it" so that she could share more loving activities with him. This was early *fall*. They were on their way. They were unstuck and full of hope.

I love my job!

...

It's *winter* and our first session was after Christmas—he wants a divorce, no discussion! Wow! I didn't see that coming, and neither did she! Kick in the stomach! Heartache!

My thoughts stray to working in the Mall selling shoes or refrigerators. What led to his change of feelings? Did he really give the "other woman" up? Or was the forbidden sex too hard to resist? Was it easier to stay in the established relationship, but he just couldn't maintain the charade?

It takes a great deal of work to rebuild a relationship after an affair. The injured party does not easily "get back to normal" once the crisis has past. Even when there is an agreement to continue the relationship, a lingering lack of trust can taint all interactions between the couple.

However, if they decide to give their relationship a genuine chance, to work hard, and stay focused on each other and on the new skills they learn in counselling, then I believe they can change and their efforts will be rewarded.

**Re-started relationships can be extremely difficult,
requiring hard work and much focus,
but they can also be most exciting and fulfilling!**

PENANCE

When you are "doing penance"* for an indiscretion and are beating yourself up for making this choice, it is appropriate for you to look and act as sorry as you feel. This is so your partner, or whomever, knows that you understand what you have done and are treating it sincerely. However, when you have reached a level where you are as sorry as you need to be—which is frequently dependent on the level of severity of your indiscretion—and you have spent an appropriate amount of time in a state of remorse, it is time to move away from the pain and forgive yourself.

Just as it is important to feel sorry for what you have done, it is equally important to stop feeling bad about something that can never be changed, even if the affected person—partner, friend, parent—is not ready to forgive you for what you have done. You decide when enough is enough and begin to resume a normal, healthy lifestyle with a relatively clear conscience.

What needs to be understood is that we can't give the *power to forgive ourselves* away to anyone else, at least not indefinitely. While healing is certainly achieved in instances where the *offended* forgives the *offender,* we must be prepared to forgive ourselves first if we expect others to forgive us as well. Penance ought not to be a permanent condition!

Remember, the length of time one does penance is not dependent on the anger/hurt of the other person, but on the level of remorse and regret of the perpetrator. When you have learned your lesson, which is the major point, from what you have done, it is time to find the courage to let go and move on.

> **Instead of feeling sorry about what was done in the past, do your appropriate penance, forgive yourself, and then do something useful in the present.**

---

* Penance feels more like a religious term than a psychological term, but seems to be an appropriate descriptor of the price one has to pay when one is *in the doghouse* with one's partner.

PEOPLE VS. ACCOMPLISHMENT

A young professional came to see me. He confided that he didn't see the need for, or obtain a "sense of accomplishment" in, playing with his only child. Because his wife was upset by his level of involvement with their child, he felt a lot of guilt. He was a good husband and provider and in many ways a good father, but he didn't "feel at all successful" when it came to spending time with his child. He felt like he needed to constantly accomplish either at work or with projects around the house. When he wasn't working, he felt that he was wasting time. I asked him to reflect more closely on his value system—to consider those things that he cherished the most. What did he prize more—relationships with people, or career/work-oriented accomplishment? While his answer was "people", his behaviour definitely reflected "accomplishment".

He understood that playing with his child was something that he valued. But at the same time, he was conflicted because he felt that painting the fence or doing a report was also very important. He was constantly in a dilemma. Which of these values would he act on?

I decided that forcing him to decide, to pick one over the other, would not be of any long-term value. I suggested that he choose to work on both of his values "on purpose". This meant that he would continue to seek out accomplishment, but would also work on building his relationship with his son, perhaps even *planning* some activities for them to do together.

Understanding without an Action Plan goes nowhere!

Like this person, many of us have grown up in families where we were taught that hard work and success are the most important values. What we need to understand is that while work is important, so is having a balance where people and relationships also count. The reason we go to work and strive for success is to have enough money to have a quality of life that includes time with our loved ones.

Some people define success by how productive they are, how much money they make or how many degrees they have acquired, instead of how "in balance" and healthy they are.

Don't confuse your career with your life.

LET'S MAKE IT OFFICIAL

He was still an emotional mess a year and a half after his affair was over. He went back to his wife because, as he said, "It was the right thing to do." After all, they had children and 23 years together.

The problem was that even though time had passed, he still passionately held on to the memories of forbidden encounters with the "other" woman.

"I haven't let go, but I need to let go, and that's why I'm here. I need your help!"

I summed up what I thought I heard him say with the least sarcastic voice I could find. "You sort of decided to go back home and you sort of decided to let the other person go, right?"

His interest was piqued. "Spot on!"

"Is sort of deciding the same as deciding?" I inquired.

"Well, no …."

"So, what you really want to do now is to say 'no' to the other woman, let her go, and say 'yes' to your wife. Have I got that straight?"

"Yes!" It was very difficult for him to sort through all the feelings about the "other woman", as well as his commitment to his wife and children. However, he appeared to be highly motivated to move beyond his "stuck" place and let the affair be a thing of the past. And he expressed that he wanted to restore the relationship with his family. He had been alone and in pain long enough, and looked forward to the healing that he felt would occur if he were to become more congruent with his values. And he did value family and the honouring of one's partner, despite having made a poor choice a year and a half before. He was now ready to do the right thing. He just needed a process.

What I proposed was an *Official Ending* to the old relationship. He was to construct an *Official Document* by writing about what was good about the "other" relationship—good memories, good feelings, etc.— and what was not so good— sneaking around, hurting his family, etc. And the third part of this assignment was to further empty all feelings about the illicit relationship into a final section called, "All It Could Have Been"—if the affair had been "right" and had continued.[4]

He was to go out and purchase an *Official Book*. In this book, he was to write the *Official Document* with a special *Official Pen*. He did all that and completed the document with, "I have Officially let you go! Goodbye!"

"If you build it, they will come."
**If you write it down,
it will help you to overcome.**

---

[4] Dan Rosin, *Communication & Relationships*, The Ewings Publishing, 2023, p.4.

"GIVING IN" ISN'T THE ANSWER

I recall that one of my clients had a real dilemma. He and his ex-wife had become deadlocked while negotiating for primary custody of their young son. His new partner had a career opportunity in another city and he was willing to pull up his roots and go with her, but only after the custody issue with his ex-wife was settled.

The new partner was not thrilled with the possibility of having an eight year old as a permanent ward. She kept saying, "I need you to make me your top priority. If you really loved me you would do this ... for me. Having an eight year old live with us full time doesn't meet my needs." This new partner remained determined in her perspective, but he loved his only child and had come too far in the custody fight with his ex to give up. I could see that this was not going to end well.

He and I had several sessions together. His partner attended once and then didn't return. In her mind, she had declared her position, thought that it was fair, and decided there was nothing else to talk about. Her mind was made up—all he had to do was abandon custody and remain content in seeing his son only on those special holidays when she decided they weren't going to go anywhere else together. At least, that's how it felt to him.

I found it very interesting to observe how this issue was finally resolved. As a result of going through this process with his new partner, what he detected in himself was fear. He was afraid that his life would become an endless series of "giving in" to her in order to prove that he loved her. His conclusion was, "I don't think I will ever be able to meet her needs, or even come close. This relationship can't only be about her. If she isn't prepared to support me on an issue as important as the custody of my child, what chance will I have with the other smaller and less important issues?"

As it happened, he didn't win full custody, but joint custody was fine with him. He didn't leave the city and his "new" partner became "old" in a hurry. His final words to me regarding his new/old partner were, "I can't love someone who doesn't love me enough to love my child." Yes!

The toughest part of maintaining a successful relationship is compromising enough so that both partners get their needs met!

YOU'RE SMOTHERING ME!

He was a serious young man trying to figure out how to have a better relationship with his girlfriend. He was confused because in the beginning of the relationship, she wanted him with her all the time. He complied and gave up most of his friends. Now she says he is *smothering* her and that he is boring. She wants out of the relationship. His question, "What happened?"

We talked and I was quite surprised at my cavalier attitude about relationships. I pontificated to the inexperienced chap:

> *Enjoy yourself, do things together, expand your horizons with a number of people, don't be exclusive until you meet that someone you just "can't let get by you" and, even then, keep a balance between this loved one, your friends and favourite activities.*

It was all very logical and totally unrealistic because, as we all know, falling in love is an emotional experience.

What I didn't take into consideration in my little diatribe was self-esteem. To a person with *low self-esteem*, every person who pays them any attention is the person they can't let get go of and will try to hang onto at all costs. The belief that they cling to in their unconscious being is that "This could be the last person who will ever pay any attention to me."

I got to thinking about the notion that we have to be so exclusive and spend all our time together as couples, that we eventually burn out on each other—single or married. Unfortunately, it is often after the burn out and some poor behaviour that couples start looking for variety in their lives. This "branching out" can either put a serious strain on the relationship, or save it!

In the beginning of a relationship, we are so willing to give up almost everything for the other person that we react to their needs and forget about our own. That's comfortable for a while, but eventually the "giving one" becomes frustrated and resentful, doesn't talk, pulls back, and oozes self-righteous anger or gets overtly angry. Remember, angry person:

> *If you don't state what you want your life to look like—and make it happen, somebody else will tell you what it should look like—and think less of you in the process.*[5]

Just because we state what we want, doesn't mean we always get what we want! However, there is a pretty good chance of never getting what we want if we never say what we want. Rather than let things happen, choose what we want our life to look like. We do not need to react to the wishes of others and call that "our path". I've heard it said that *wishy-washy isn't sexy.*

Know what you want from your life, establish goals, set direction for yourself, and understand that if the relationship is going to work, you will need to learn how to assist your partner to get their needs met as well. You certainly will need to learn the "art of negotiating".

Your partner is very different than you, with different needs and goals. How well you listen and compromise will determine the eventual success of the relationship.

Two strong and self-sufficient "I"s make an incredible "We".
I choose to have you in my life, but you aren't my whole life.
I want you close, but I also want time separate from you.

---

[5] Rosin, *Finding Balance*, p. 59.

TASKS VS. PEOPLE

He was taught from an early age that the "only" way to complete a task or assignment was the "correct" way. Throughout his life, he had focused on tasks (a spin off on "accomplishment") with a kind of dogmatic, perfectionist plodding. Unfortunately, he began to notice a trend—the completion of *tasks* became more important than his relationships with *people*.

This lack of concern for people did not go unnoticed and was damaging his relationships. He constantly rubbed people the wrong way and pushed them away. His emphasis was on tasks first and people second, or third or ….

This led to the following dichotomy:

TASK ONLY	Results in	LACK OF CONCERN FOR PEOPLE
Focus on the task and get strokes for perfection and completion		*Push people* away and then feel frustrated and angry with them them for not liking you

He unhappily stated that this dichotomous existence was no longer working for him. It became clear to him that by making tasks the only option in his life and people secondary, he was lonely and unhappy.

If he decided that people were important, then he would need to learn how to acknowledge them, to have differences with them, without walking away or discounting them. He wasn't excited about this.

He had believed all his life that he was only acceptable as a person when he completed tasks. And since he had chosen to have as little to do with people as possible, he found himself increasingly frustrated and angry, both with himself and others, because he felt so alone.

As a result of the task-oriented focus of his upbringing and his conviction that "I am no good with people", he had proven his belief true (self-fulfilling prophecy), and as a result there were no people in his life who cared about him. However, this situation was now in conflict with a new desire to spend time in the company of others. A real dilemma!

His challenge:
TASKS ------ NO ------ PEOPLE
TASKS ------ OR ------ PEOPLE
TASKS ------ AND ------ PEOPLE

I believe it is possible to get things done (tasks) and still have healthy relationships. When we come from dysfunctional families—and who doesn't—as adults we need to consciously make different decisions than what we learned from or how we survived our *Family of Origin.** We now have power; we can now choose!

Tasks and People was his choice!

We can choose to work only on tasks and push people away, or to work on tasks and caringly interact with people. No matter what we were taught or how we chose to survive at an early age, we now have a choice how we live life as an adult.

The following words were written on the tomb of an Anglican Bishop (1100 A.D.) in the Crypts of Westminster Abbey:

---

*   "Family of Origin" is the family one is born into.

When I was young and free and my imagination had no limits, I dreamed of changing the world. As I grew older and wiser, I discovered the world would not change, so I shortened my sights somewhat and decided to change only my country. But it, too, seemed immovable. As I grew into my twilight years, in one last desperate attempt, I settled for changing only my family, those closest to me, but alas, they would have none of it. And now as I lie on my deathbed, I suddenly realize: If I had only changed myself first, then by example I would have changed my family. From their inspiration and encouragement, I would then have been able to better my country and, who knows, I may have even changed the world.

– Anonymous

I MEET YOU AND THEN I GIVE UP MY FRIENDS?

I am often asked by my female clients, "Why, when I meet a man, do I give up my friends and become exclusively dependent on that relationship? Before we met, my life had 'order'. I did the things I wanted to do when I wanted to do them. I had fun. I felt on track. I was being me! And then as soon as I met him, it all changed .... I start a relationship and then a month or two into it, I can't find me. I am willing to do whatever he wants to fulfill his needs so he won't leave me. It's funny, but he doesn't seem to worry about me leaving him. I'm not happy. In fact, I am miserable, wondering and worrying if he will continue to 'pick me'. Somewhere I stopped being me. The 'me' who was the very person he was first attracted to. I become someone I think I need to be to have him stay in my life." Hmm!

I encourage women to stop asking "Why do I do this (change to suit my partner)", and start checking out the family models in their life. Look at the values of their mother/grandmother around this issue, and study the messages women have received throughout history as part of their training in a "man's world".

Since women were made to feel inferior and expected to take responsibility for the success or failure of all relationships, it is no mystery why they try so hard to make relationships work—even bad ones. They *have to* make it work. They have been conditioned to believe it is their fault if the relationship fails. Their self-esteem is inextricably tied to the success of the relationship.

Then there is the "I don't want to be alone" issue. In spite of the pain of a bad relationship, individuals continue to struggle. They try their best to make the unworkable work because they fear this is it, this is all they get, no one else will ever choose them and they will indeed be alone.

I have trouble understanding the kind of thinking that allows a person to continue in a bad relationship, rather than be alone. As a therapist, I realize how difficult and emotionally draining it is to leave a relationship—finances, kids, family expectations, and pressure to stay. However, my belief is we only have this one life, and so are we really willing to sacrifice it in a bad relationship? I am not talking about bailing out because it's just too difficult, but I am talking about leaving because it is unworkable.

On the 10-Point Scale, where 1 is low (we receive nothing from the relationship, are perpetually unhappy, and feel no hope that it will get better) and 10 is ideal, many who have left their partner, place themselves at around 7 or 8, when in their previous relationship they saw themselves—yes, in hindsight—at a 3 or 4. Not only did the relationship fail to enhance their lives, it actually took the joy right out of it.

Stop asking "Why do I give all my power to my partner?" and start asking "What do I want from my life?" Then start working toward that. Be an 8, be "in charge" of your life! Be discerning and only allow other 8s into your life.

Be aware of the "4" (wolf) in an "8" (sheep's) clothing.
Stop rescuing 4s and thinking you can make them into an 8.

LOVE SONGS (poem)

*Why can't people realize
that love first means love of self.
How can I possibly love others,
how can I tune into their
love energy – if I can't
tune into mine.
To understand love,
you must have
experienced pain, joy,
loneliness, acceptance,
failure, success,
not in surface proportions
but to its depths.*

*Love is not a mind
exercise. It is a
totality, a wholeness.
So then if I am going to
sing love songs, I had
better listen to my
feelings about me, turn
back to my experience,
let the world strike the
chords inside me.*

D. Rosin

"NOTHING OR ALL" PRINCIPLE

This was the fourth long-term relationship that had "not worked out". She chose men who were, in her words, "emotionally unavailable" to her. She was confused and angry with herself for focusing on a vision of what she wanted the relationship to look like, instead of what her partner's behaviour was actually presenting.

She was clear on the principle that sex was only allowed in a relationship if you were going to get married. She pronounced, "I am a good little Catholic girl and I have always lived my life based on that value." My question to her was, "So, once you have sex with your partner, are you then committed to him for life?" She looked a little bewildered, but hesitatingly answered, "Yes." I drew my version of her "Vision Cycle" on the blackboard:

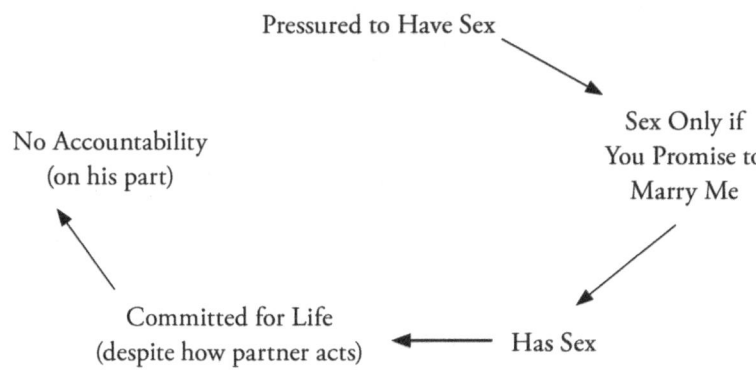

She realized something was terribly wrong with her thinking and the resultant cycle she had created. It was the "All or Nothing" principle in reverse. To summarize, she would treat her partners as follows: "You get nothing, no sex until you promise me marriage, and then you get it all, forever, in spite of how you treat me."* Guess what they promised? And guess what never happened!

NOTHING	SEX	ALL
(no sex, no commitment)	(the promise of marriage)	(sex, total commitment, but no accountability for his behaviour)

Her vision was locked in and overrode the reality of the experience with her partner. No matter what her partner did, she would not confront him about his behaviour. She gave up her "personal power" because of her value, which was, "Once she had sex/promise of marriage, she was committed for life". From then on she refused to see the flaws in the relationship,[6] to act on unacceptable behaviours, or to administer reasonable consequences commensurate with her partner's actions. She gave in and gave up, and her partners left anyway.

Somewhere between giving NOTHING (no commitment) and giving ALL (total commitment with no accountability) lies the most appropriate responses.

---

* It seemed that if she heard "I love you" (marriage), then having sex in this context was okay—she was not a bad person.

[6] Rosin, *Communication & Relationships*, p. 16.

BLINDED BY THE VISION

As I eluded to in the "Nothing or All" Principle, we make people fit our "vision"—thoughts, hopes, dreams—of what we think or feel a good relationship should look like, instead of what it really is. We see what we want to see. This is particularly true in the beginning of our relationship when we let the undesirable behaviours slide because we want this person and this relationship to work. As I stated in the aforementioned concept[7], our vision takes priority over reality. We will make that round peg fit in the square hole, no matter what!

Take your left hand and move it directly in front of your face and eyes. Place your right hand at arm's length in front of your left but also in front of your face and eyes. The left hand prevents you from being able to clearly see the right hand. In a relationship, your vision of what you want the other person to be prevents you from seeing the person as they actually are.

There is a fine line between following one's hopes and dreams, and having those same hopes and dreams blind us to the reality of unacceptable behaviour. We need to set aside our vision and be free to confront and change that which is not in our best interest.

In the heat of one's passions and desires, it is often easy to be led astray by the mirage on the horizon—those things that seem to be real until we get closer and realize they aren't there. Make sure your vision is focused on the objects that are there, and not obstructed by the things that "should be" or that we "desire to be" there.

Be careful not to focus so intently on the positive fiction of your hopes and dreams that it blinds you to the negative reality of what is actually happening.

---

[7] Rosin, *Communication & Relationships*, p. 16.

BACKYARD (CONT.)

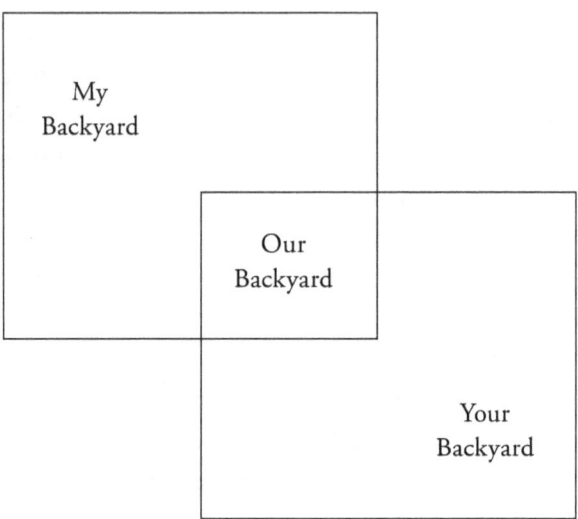

When I first introduced the Backyard concept,[8] my understanding of it was rather narrow and somewhat sexist. I restricted the concept to merely "doings" and not "feelings". I focused on: *She* – sewing, visiting, working out; *He* – golfing, working on his car, playing pool; *Ours* – working on the house together, vacations, visiting. Consequently, I missed stating the most important message inherent in this concept.

Activities are good and we need them to have a full life. However, it is now my understanding that it takes more than activities to keep a relationship "on track" and healthy. The real key is the *attitude* each partner has about working hard at enhancing the other partner's life.

It's not just how many activities you do together, but your attitudes toward each other. It is your individual willingness to put energy into the relationship, to enhance your partner's life, to provide what the other needs, to be personally fulfilled, and to see that you both get what you

---

[8] Rosin, *Finding Balance* p. 73.

need to feel loved and cared about. And to do so in a spirit that says to your partner, "You are Number One in my life."

It is important that we ask daily what we can both do to make each other's lives better, and then keep that thought foremost on our minds.*

> **"Doing" things and having fun together is what makes a relationship worthwhile—today! Exhibiting a "positive spirited attitude" toward one's partner is the long-term glue that keeps the relationship together—over time!**

---

* I believe that both partners have to work equally hard at the relationship. However, if things get off track and one partner needs to step up and reach out, I do feel that in most cases it should be the male who considers this behaviour. I know I am in trouble with the males, but being one, I have some insight into this matter. Consequently, I base my decision on the fact that most of the time—but not always, and I certainly will stand corrected on a case by case basis—it is the men who find themselves disproportionately represented on the "self-centred" side of the continuum. Besides, somebody has to set the ball rolling in a positive direction, so why not the men!

DYSFUNCTIONAL FAMILY FALLOUT

When she first came to see me, she was carrying around a great deal of resentment and hostility. She had recently concluded that the majority of her problems in her adult life were the result of "… never having been loved as a young person" because her "parents did not know how to show love".

She hung on to this sad fact as if it was a permission slip to get out of gym class, to not have to accept responsibility for her behaviour in the present because of their behaviour in the past. Her truth was that her parents were quite verbally abusive toward her. And while I agree that a great deal of behaviour later in life is due to the experiences we have early on, I said that she shouldn't feel especially unique since most people come from dysfunctional families.

According to Virginia Satir, John Bradshaw and other leading family therapists and authors, between 95 and 100% of North Americans come from families described as dysfunctional. Certainly, most of us have had the misfortune of coming from one of these unhealthy, *dysfunctional* families—"I never received enough love (*strokes**) as a young person; my father was an alcoholic; I was physically abused; nobody really cared." All terrible experiences that leave scars and result in acting out and driven kinds of behaviours.

I often state, "Given your past, your behaviour is understandable. But in the present, now that you are an adult with power and choice, those behaviours are no longer acceptable." It is not acceptable to continue to be locked into these antiquated feelings and thoughts.

---

*   A stroke is a unit of recognition.

There comes a time when we need to realize the impact of these early experiences, talk about them, own them, and then let them go. In our minds and through our actions, we need to stop playing back the tapes of these early negative experiences. We must refuse to use them to justify present feelings and behaviours.

To some degree the same goes for past positive accomplishments that get replayed instead of creating new ones. Our past needs to be just that—our past.

For us to make the transition from the past to the present, we need to establish a new criterion for obtaining the love and fulfillment we failed to receive from our Family of Origin.[9] Instead of focusing on dys-functional family memories and directives, which result in compensating behaviours such as extreme accomplishment or drivenness and rescuing, we need to focus on health and well-being[10].

Your behaviour is understandable, but no longer appropriate!

> *Some families are definitely more dysfunctional than others. To those people who survived the extremes and find this simplistic solution disrespectful, I apologize. There is a wide variation in problems and methods of treatment for every individual who has survived a dysfunctional environment. I don't mean to imply that in order to achieve peace and healing all one has to do is just decide to feel "different". Releasing pain from the past is very hard work and needs to be undertaken consciously. What I intend to emphasize above all else is that life is about choices. And often, that means refusing to accept the consequences that come through the choices that others made for us while we were growing up.*

---

[9] Rosin, *Finding Balance*, p. 92.
[10] Rosin, *Finding Balance*, p. 5.

STOP THE HURT AND MOVE ON!

You can't continue to love someone who doesn't love you!

How wide is the gap between loving a person—including professing you *can't live* without them and will *absolutely die* if they reject you—to hating them if they don't return your love?

> *"There's always one to turn and walk*
> *away and one who just wants to stay.*
> *But who said that love is always fair,*
> *and why should I care?"*
>
> *("Why Should I Care?", Clint Eastwood)*

When a relationship ends, invariably one person tries to keep it alive. They feel great variances in hope and hurt as they try to make sense of the break-up. Unfortunately, severed relationships rarely heal to the point where the ex-partners can become friends or lovers again. They rarely heal in a manner that is healthy; in fact, the hurt often becomes even more intense after the break-up. Along with this intensity, there is confusion, grief, and the fading of hope. Eventually, the person gets tired of hurting, *lets go* of what was, and decides to *move on*. And that is good; that is reality.

Sometimes, however, the hurt doesn't go away and people harbour it for a very long time. Rather than deal with the hurt, some find themselves on the rebound in a new relationship before completing the grieving process, while others get back into "the dating game", but hold on to the memory of "the one that left", and it gets in their way. People who bury the hurt and allow it to dominate future relationships can inflict all sorts of pain on unsuspecting significant others who have done nothing wrong, nothing to offend.

I believe that when you *hurt* more than you *hope,* eventually a shift will occur. It seems that most humans cannot exist for very long with "hurt" before they need to get themselves out from under that feeling, and the process of "letting go" begins.

**You can't continue to love someone who doesn't love you!
"Letting go" and "moving on" are required to stop
the "hurt" of a broken relationship.**

"HE'S BACK WITH THE RED HEAD"

He came into my office with a hung-dog look. "No matter what I do, she finds fault," he uttered.

We began several sessions in which this client explored—complained about—his relationship with his wife of seven years. He painted a picture that exposed her as a *cold* and *controlling* woman who made all the decisions and left him in the dark about most things. He was relegated to acting as the kids' chauffeur and being the household's chef-in-residence—breakfast, lunch and supper. He lamented that he couldn't even "go drinking with friends on Friday night without her making a snide comment".

I could empathize with his plight, but his goal in coming to therapy was not entirely clear to me. It seemed that all of the problems were entirely outside of himself.

I asked to meet his wife. Not surprisingly, she saw things very differently from how he saw them. She presented herself as a *strong* and *responsible* woman who was forced to make most of the decisions because "he was invisible". As she explained, "Even when he is around, he isn't there and he's not around much."

Each saw the other as the problem. They came in together for several sessions, during which no great insights occurred and I wasn't doing back flips at their progress. Still, they did their homework and seemed to pay better attention to each other. And then it happened.

She telephoned and simply said that it was over! "He told me he has no sexual feelings for me," she confided. That was bad enough, but then came the curve ball that I really didn't see coming. *"He's back with the red head*; in fact he's been with her the whole time we have been in counselling."

As I dove for my notes of our past sessions, I was thinking to myself, I don't remember anyone mentioning a red head. Nine sessions and there's a red head stashed in the closet and nobody mentions her to the therapist?! Of course, it didn't help that I didn't ask.

While I was still recovering, he surprised me by making an appointment for himself. He laid it all out—the affair, the loss of love for his wife, his struggle to give up the red head, and the lies in therapy. He wasn't a terrible fellow, just didn't have many relationship skills. He got one last thought from me before we concluded:

> *For a person to feel healthy sexual feelings toward a long-time partner, that person needs to communicate a great deal of warmth, caring, concern and generosity toward their partner. Their partner is then motivated to reciprocate those feelings and it begins to get exciting again.*

He wasn't buying it!

After our last session, I reflected on all our sessions and my disappointment at having missed such a significant factor in this couple's relationship. The presence of the *other person* completely eluded me!

And then I told myself what I would have told my clients if they kept beating themselves up—*Let it go!* It's not easy to understand why he would repeatedly state, "I really want to work on this relationship" when at the same time he was visiting the red head—who apparently had "huge boobs", according to his wife. What was perplexing is that the guy paid me to sit and listen to him lie.

I am always saddened when a relationship ends. I often find myself at a loss for words to the partner who has been left behind. My immediate thoughts were, "Just how is a wife with three kids, who works nights to pay for an advanced music program for the eldest child, supposed to compete with a red head with …?" Well, you get the picture.

For that matter, how is therapy supposed to help someone make their life better when in their mind they are already living out their fantasy? Can't!

Remember:

The person who feels the least amount of spark, needs to work the hardest to rekindle that spark!

FULFILLMENT

I often find myself with clients who identify themselves as depressed, and/or experiencing feelings of having missed out in life, talking about fulfillment.

I do believe that many people have an expectation that their job is going to fulfill them, and in some cases it does—partly! That having a relationship, or a family, or having a nice car/house will fulfill then, and it does—partly!

All of these relationships and things do count, but there is a piece of us that just won't be satisfied by being in a relationship or by acquiring possessions. That piece is *"fulfillment"*.

To me, fulfillment is a very personal thing. We need to find out what that unique thing about us is; that thing we have a passion for that is just ours. Perhaps for you it is learning, music, exercise, golf, painting, animals, grandchildren, special relationships, higher power, or helping others.

> **When you're looking to feel fulfilled**
> **Don't start with reality.**
> **Start with the possibilities and dreams**
> **Then temper with reality.**

SHE'S A KEEPER

Start by being a "keeper" yourself.

Stay concerned with what fulfills your partner (see Fulfillment, previous concept). Don't demand that he/she stop doing what they love doing, that which fulfills them, (music, art restoration, sports, video games—all in moderation of course), to be more available to you. You are important to your partner and vice-versa, but if you demand that their passionate activities be curtailed, you will soon have a resentful partner on your hands.

The young lady sat down and with much anger in her eyes shared with me, "It's over, my relationship is over." I sympathized and asked what had made her come to this decision. "Well, he bought a small TV and put it in the basement to watch sports!"

I was thinking, *okay, so what's the problem here,* and I asked "So, what's the problem here?" Her face showed mild surprise, like it was so obvious, why did I even need to bother to ask. "He's downstairs watching sports instead of sitting with me upstairs and watching 'our' shows."

"Our" shows. My mind did a complete flip and heard "my " shows—but I ignored that thought and kept on listening. "In the summer, it's about the time he spends golfing." Once again I rushed ahead in my thoughts and because I know guys who do this—3-4 times a week at the golf course, a few beers after the game and it's 5-6 hours before they get home. She explained, "He goes golfing every Saturday with my dad and a few friends and I just sit at home. "I'm thinking, once a week and with your dad! This guy sounds pretty considerate for a guy.

Then she described the offence that really clarified her decision to leave. "He plays hockey late at night and I'm always sitting at home by myself." So I am thinking again, maybe he is one of those guys who goes drinking and a hockey game breaks out, you know 3-4 times a week. Nope! Once a week, Friday, late game 11-12 PM. This guy is a saint and is putting all the rest of us males to shame. Not so in her mind.

I realized as I was talking to this person that perception is what drives the bus. My thoughts are driven by comparisons to what I have experienced previously in my life, what I believe to be true. Her perceptions and beliefs were very different than mine and absolutely correct for her.

My question to her was somewhat along the lines of, "So you see in these times when he is out doing his thing (being fulfilled) as taking time away from you and the relationship?"

"Yes, and this TV in the basement is the final straw!"

I did my best to calmly share what I thought was a "real world" perspective of how we need to do things outside of the relationship, things that bring us pleasure and fulfillment. I'm afraid she wasn't in any mood to listen. Her session—her perspective!

She was going to change him and have him upstairs on the sofa with her watching "our" shows or the relationship was over. Her idea of her partner being fulfilled was that he would have the same sense of enjoyment from the same activities as she or he "didn't want a relationship with her very badly!"

Some guys, and I suppose gals as well, do cross the line of "fulfillment" and enter into "selfish" territory—that being getting their needs met at others' expense. Of course I don't advocate this kind of behaviour. However, I did feel this person was selfishly imposing her vision of what she thought the relationship should be on him and I definitely saw big trouble on the horizon for this couple.

> **I remember telling my friends about**
> **how my wife encourages my golfing/music/writing**
> **because I love it and it's good for me.**
> **They tell me and it reinforces what I have**
> **always known, She's a Keeper**

93% OF COMMUNICATION ...

I have heard it said that 93% of communication is *tone, inflection* and *body posture*, and that only 7% is *content*.

A client and I were discussing the various aspects of communication and the impact of poor communication on relationships. She was very succinct and firm in how she spoke. She saw herself as an honest and "to the point" individual, and was quite upset at how she was perceived by her colleagues.

As we talked, it became clear that what she saw as honest and "to the point" in herself, others saw as judgemental and dogmatic. "People seem to be standoffish, even mad at me," she lamented. What I heard in her tone and inflection, even though she never actually used the words, were the "should" and "have to" inferences for others. Her words were benign, but how she delivered them—tone, inflection, body posture— left little mystery as to how she truly felt things should be done.

She and I agreed that when we communicate it is very difficult to hide our inner thoughts and directives. Our choice of words and how we deliver our message generally makes it pretty clear what our "intent" is. We need to learn to listen better—Active Listening—and to speak— tone, inflection, body posture—without inviting the listener to feel they have to defend themselves.

Good *active listening* says, "I care about you, and will respectfully listen to you, even if I do not agree with what you say."

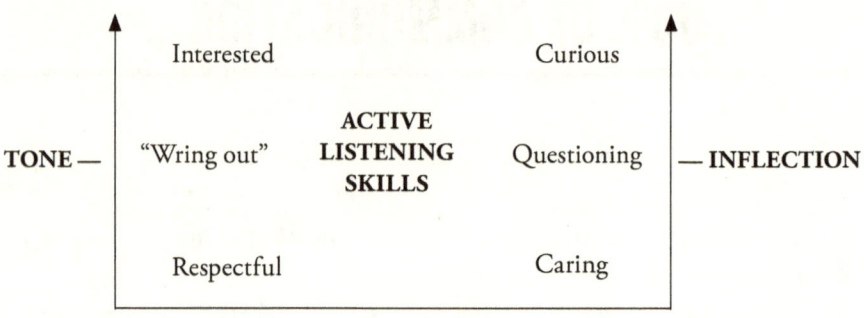

Communication—Listening and Speaking— is a package—tone, inflection, body posture and content. It's not always what you say, but how you say it. Your tone, inflection and body posture become the message.

"YOU" LANGUAGE

He was talking about how he continually beat himself up so as to prevent anyone else from doing so!

We were discussing Communication Theory 101—listening and speaking—and to demonstrate his poor communication skills, he kept interjecting examples of where and how he "screwed up". It was his belief that he needed to put himself down before someone else did. He told me that this discounting of self came from an internal voice, which was a product of the people and experiences he had earlier in his life.

The way he described it, there were people in his past who had judged him, were overly critical of who he was and what he did, and who modelled negativity. They encouraged him to be down on himself and on his life until their messages took on a life of their own—an inner voice.

During the course of my sessions with people such as this client, I have found that the language common to self-deprecation is *"you"* language. This language takes the form of a blaming, dumping language that further erodes one's self-esteem. *"You"* language is often the first language learned in the environment where you grew up—family, school, church, community.

When we are confronted with *"you"* language in these settings, we feel blamed, less important, incompetent, dumb, and we develop a self-limiting script.[11] Later in life, we then use this "you" language to put others down before they put us down, and to put ourselves down before they put us down—in other words, we beat them to the punch!

Unfortunately, a negative script[12] developed in childhood establishes entrenched patterns throughout our adult life. It's bad enough that the

---

[11] Eric Berne, *What do you say after you say hello?* New York, NY, Grove Press, 1972, p. 25.

[12] Berne, *What do you say ...* p. 25.

child[13] experienced such putdowns at all, let alone having to repeat them over and over again—to themselves—now as an adult!

> **A Life Script written early—sometimes by age 3 to 5—can be rewritten! We can re-decide, based on more current and up-to-date information—the ability to think rationally— that we are okay and capable of much more than our early script would allow.**

---

[13] Eric Berne, *Games People Play,* New York, NY, Grove Press, 1964, p. 23.

THE OTHER PERSON'S TRUTH

In my previous book, I introduced the concept that nobody has Universal Truth.[14] We only have our own perception of the truth and yet we foolishly spend an inordinate amount of time trying to convince others that the way we see things is the correct way.

Many of my clients have admitted that they have stopped listening to their partners and spend most of their interpersonal energy trying to convince them that "My way is the correct/better way." They have stopped listening and started blaming. Even worse, they have given up and say nothing, give nothing, and only want to be left alone. Their language is "You are always …" and "You make me so mad when you …", and things never get better between them. Where do we start to make things better? Hmm! Do we give up? I don't think so!

If "giving up" means giving up your belief that you have Universal Truth, that your way is the correct and only way, then yes, give up!

But what I advocate instead is to stop promoting—share don't sell—your position and instead respect and acknowledge the other person's point of view. You don't have to agree with each other, but you do have to respect your partner's perception, and anyone else's perception, and their right to have that perception.

One way communication? No thanks!

Remember:

Differences are strengths, not something to be afraid of.

Someone who sees the world differently than you do, isn't necessarily stupid, stubborn or dangerous—just different!

---

[14] Rosin, *Finding Balance*, p. 84.

Be proud of who you are and how you see the world—thoughts, feelings, values and beliefs—but also allow others to be proud of who they are and how they see the world.

In a relationship, differences are something to be respected and cherished, not something to be attacked or changed.

MEN AND WOMEN ARE DIFFERENT, SO LET'S STOP MAKING SUCH A BIG DEAL OF IT!

In an interpersonal relationship, we don't need to see things the same as our partner in order for the relationship to be successful.

We spend so much time trying to convince people, including our partner, that the way we see the world—how we think, feel, value and believe—is how they should also see the world. We spend hours, days, and even decades, arguing and fighting about who is right and trying to win.

After centuries of working with couples—at least it feels that way!—it is now my understanding that when we accept others only because they see things the same way we do, or when we feel a need to convince someone that we have the correct perspective and that they need to change their own way of seeing things to mirror our own, then we definitely have a problem.

If the other person does comply out of frustration or fear, they will sabotage the relationship somewhere down the line. Conversation and the relationship will become a competition, like a football game that someone is trying to win so as to impose his or her will over the other person. In an interpersonal relationship, "winners" are not revered, they are to be gotten even with!

Men and women, and even persons of the same sex, are different from each other. And this needs to be acceptable. Often, there is no attempt to understand these differences on either side. For some very real reasons, we humans have a need to convince each other that how we see things is either the correct way, or the only way. The modus operandi becomes, "I need you to see things my way for me to feel okay, to be in control. If you will only change by adopting my perspective, then I will feel more worthy." With many couples, the game becomes, "Whoever is loudest and longest or most silent and withdrawn, wins."

As the famous book title states, *Men Are From Mars, Women Are From Venus*.[15] So, let's just accept that and stop trying to change each other. Become a better listener. Be more respectful and curious about your differences. And stop trying to mould your partner into your own image.

Remember, in a relationship,
if you have a winner and a loser,
you will eventually have two losers.

---

[15] John Gray, *Men Are From Mars, Women Are From Venus*. New York, NY, Harper Collins, 1992.

DON'T FIGHT—EXPRESS!

When you are in a relationship, "winning" ought not to be in your vocabulary. Fighting and arguing are all about somebody trying to win or be in control. In my years of counselling couples, I have found that success in a relationship is generally achieved when there is freedom to express one's self and be heard, along with a genuine willingness to really listen.[16]

Learn to state your *Thoughts, Feelings, Values and Beliefs* (TFVB)[17]— and be proud of them! And then also be proud of your partner's TFVB, even if they are different to yours. Stop being so dogmatic when it comes to your own opinions and perceptions. After all, it's not like you have the inside track on all the "right" answers anyway; you only have the right answers for yourself.

Of course, it is important to express yourself, but not with the tone of voice that says, "This is the only way to see this issue, (*stupid!*)." How else will the other person interpret your tone than as a put down or challenge? And once it has been received, the "fight will really be on". Instead, adopt the tone that says, "This is the way *I* see it, how do *you* see it?" and allow both parties to express themselves, be heard and feel respected. There is no need to fight or argue when you feel respected.

You don't need to win, or even agree with your partner, but you always need to be respectful.

---

[16] Rosin, *Finding Balance*, p. 88.
[17] Rosin, *Finding Balance*, p. 53.

DON'T GO FOR THE WIN—DISCUSS

It was our first session, and after about 20 minutes of high-level tension and verbal jousting between this couple, I had my turn to speak.

"So, fighting and arguing is what you do?"

"Yes!"

"It's not so much that you want to win the argument, but that you can't stand losing to your partner, right?"

"Yes!"

"Did you know that when you 'go for the win', that when you argue and fight, you actually stop listening to your partner and focus only on getting your point across?"

"Um, no."

Fighting and arguing generally means that one or both partners are going for the win. In other words, they are trying to have their perspective accepted as the "correct" way of seeing or doing things. *Charm, anger, intellectual persuasion, coldness and intimidation* are the tools used by the "fight master" to bring people around to their way of seeing things.

Seeing it "my way" is what is meant by "winning". Not seeing it "my way" is considered a rejection. Fighting and arguing is often driven by low self-esteem, fear of rejection, and the need for control. Because of this, it has a tendency to become a self-serving activity in that you only hear yourself. Instead of *actively listening*[18] to the other person, you actively push your own agenda.

Good communication is not about winning. It's about *listening*, and *speaking* in a way so as not to invite the other person to feel they have to

---

[18] Rosin, *Finding Balance*, p. 47.

be defensive. It's about respecting the other person's perspective— while, of course, maintaining respect for your own. It is important to understand that nobody has "Universal Truth",[19] and therefore it should be possible to feel that *I am okay and you are okay*, even when we disagree.

It is interesting that many of my clients *know* the basics of communication, but don't practise what they know. They are often very proficient communicators at their workplace or in their profession. However, they don't use what they know at home with their partner and children. My hunch is they are too fatigued from an overworked lifestyle to concentrate on proper communication. Or they feel they have been treated unfairly—partner, children—and react with a short fuse or just shut down. The joy of *listening* to or being *heard* by someone who cares is replaced by "What's the sense in talking? We only end up arguing." And both parties feel worse.

Every person enjoys being and needs to be *heard*. They need a chance to *express* themselves without being judged or discounted. You don't have to agree with everyone, but if you want to be close to them, you do have to respect their perspectives—including their thoughts, feelings, values and beliefs. You have to really listen to them.

---

[19] Rosin, *Finding Balance*, p. 84.

Unhealthy and Dysfunctional	**Healthy and Functional**
Fight/Argue Win/Lose	Discussion Win/Win
My way of thinking is the correct way	Practise respectful "Active Listening" and use "I" language
Involves:	**Involves:**
Using whatever means to win – mean-spirited put-downs, sarcasm, name calling, swearing, bringing up the past. Tone of voice can be threatening, loud, intimidating, cold or falsely charming.	We hear each other's position, but that doesn't mean we agree with that position. We don't force our agenda, we share it. Tone of voice is gentle and non-threatening.

**Discussion—You Talk, I Listen, I Acknowledge;
I Talk, You Listen, You Acknowledge**

ALL PERSPECTIVES ARE EQUAL, BUT MINE IS MORE EQUAL

When locked in "mortal" combat with one's partner on an issue, do you: 1) give up and give in, 2) never give up and "go for the win", or 3) accept that is how your partner sees it, that they have a right to their perspective, and that you also have a right to your perspective? In certain instances in life, you need to reconcile your own views with another person's position, such as when a decision needs to be made involving both of you. In these cases, the skills of *negotiating* and *compromising* must be utilized.

I see many couples start a downward spiral in their relationship where one is worn out and giving up, and the other is still working on *winning*. Even though their history can show them that this way of responding to each other does not work, it too often becomes the way of communicating with each other and is *locked-in* through repetition.

Eventually, they tire of this quality of communication, and either desire to achieve resolution to their many issues, or they simply wish to get away from the other person. This is often the stage of the relationship when I get to see them and, unfortunately, it's often too late for the relationship to be saved.

I have found from counselling these couples that when someone lives for a long enough period of time in a relationship where their needs aren't being met and they are told over and over again that they are wrong in how they think, they eventually become hostile and resort to blaming the other person. Their anger is very righteous in that they can now blame the other person for the total failure of the relationship, instead of taking responsibility for their own share of inappropriate behaviours.

Blaming others for our own poor behaviour is not all that uncommon. I believe most of us learn to respond this way when growing up as kids in our Family of Origin. "I wouldn't have to yell and scream if you would …." I'm sorry, but that is a crock!

We alone are responsible for what comes out of our mouths and how we react. We are also responsible for listening to others and accepting their views as their truth.

The most important principle to learn when confronted by another's perspective is to recognize that *all perspectives are equal.* In those times when someone else's perspective conflicts with our own, enough to invite us to become angry or upset or emotional, we must hold the following tenet foremost in our minds: "You can invite me to be angry, upset, whatever, but you can't make me be any of those things. Only I can choose how I behave."

In a relationship, the decision becomes one of choosing to be respectful, to be non-judgemental, to be calm, and to be accepting of our differences. When we invest in practising these principles, the returns are often much greater than the effort used to make the investment.

Stop needing to "win"—work on your own self-esteem— and learn to be more respectful of how other people see the world.

CONFRONTATION AND ITS RELATIONSHIP TO WINNING

Arguments and fights often occur because "someone is trying to win". (Oh, have I said that before?) One or both partners are interested in having their point of view accepted as the one that is "correct".[20] As a result, instead of listening to what is being shared, the person is *rehearsing* their response, which inflames what is already a problematic mode of communication. Winning becomes the goal; respecting the other person's perspective is no longer important.

There is a saying that I share at least once with every couple I work with: "In a relationship when you have a winner and a loser, eventually you will have two losers." Couples engage in the angry game of "whoever is loudest and endures the longest, wins". To the winner, beware—at some point, the loser will get even!

Anger is not only used to win the point, but in many cases, the angry person will then blame the other person for "having to get angry in order to make you understand".

While confrontational styles, win–lose dynamics and anger are all significant barriers to effective communication in a relationship, the situation becomes even more complex when self-esteem is thrown into the mix. I believe that people with high self-esteem are less interested in winning and more generous with praise and forgiveness. They feel confident about themselves and in who they are, even if they aren't successful at controlling the interactions with their significant other.

For someone with high self-esteem, a discussion consists of: "I have a point of view, you have a point of view; you talk, I listen; I talk, you listen; I'm okay, you're okay."

---

[20] Rosin, *Finding Balance,* p. 88.

By contrast, people with low or no self-esteem either allow themselves to be manipulated into a powerless position or can only feel okay when they win. They either say nothing or come across as aggressive. Neither way is effective.

> *Whoever is louder and longer or colder and more sullen, wins. Not true! Communication ceases when respect gets eroded and a defeatist "what's the sense in talking to you" attitude is developed, generally by the person who loses most often.*

SO WHAT WOULD I HAVE TO DO?

People in relationships often play what is called the *Blame Game*. I blame you, you blame me. I judge you, you judge me.

A similar and equally destructive game is the Keeping Score or *Points Game*. It is where we allocate points to our partner's behaviour and then cash those points in for a guilt-free dump on the person. "You were mean to me last week, so I will have a guilt-free temper tantrum or shopping spree this week." The big danger with this game is we feel justified in treating our partner poorly and don't feel any remorse for our actions. This game escalates quickly.

The problem is, as long as we are locked into this ridiculous game of blaming, neither one of us will get our needs met. Instead, we will have to settle for much less than what is possible in a truly respectful and loving relationship.

What can be done to break this dysfunctional game that ends up in gridlock? What can be done so the other person can once again see you as a warm and caring individual, like in your early years together? Who starts the *reaching out* process of making a couple healthy once again?

The ideal answer is "we" will. That is, both of you will reach out and work on this relationship simultaneously. But if only one of you feels motivated at this time, then "I" will is a start.

Stop blaming. Start acting respectfully before it's too late!

DISCUSSION/CONVERSATION: THE BUILDING BLOCKS OF COMMUNICATION

In my previous book, I introduced Active Listening[21] and Speaking[22] as the primary components of communication— two skill sets that can be practised separately. I left it at that, merely introducing the two units as the requirements for good communication.

What I have come to understand in the intervening time is that we don't have a *communication*, per se. Rather, communication is broken into units called discussion topics, which join together to produce *conversation*. A *discussion* is a unit of verbal talk on a particular topic. The rule that holds this unit together is simply:

You talk—I listen, I Acknowledge (Y — I — IA)
I talk—You listen, You acknowledge (I — Y —YA)
Your turn—My turn.

Diagrammatically, a discussion does not look as sexy as a DNA molecule; it looks more like a string of wieners: You talk – I listen, I acknowledge what you said, then I talk – You listen, you acknowledge and so on.

$$\boxed{Y\text{-}I\text{-}IA} \longrightarrow \boxed{I\text{-}Y\text{-}YA}$$

A *conversation* is a number of these discussion topics—and resultant thoughts, feelings, values and beliefs—run together in a respectful manner. Conversation with its ebb and flow, give and take, is at the heart of human interaction. Conversation is the medium through which communication occurs.

---

[21] Rosin, *Finding Balance*, p. 47.
[22] Rosin, *Finding Balance*, p. 53.

Communication is an art form.
Discussion—"Listener–Speaker"—Units are the building blocks of conversation. Conversation is a series of these many units strung together with feeling so they flow into what is referred to as "meaningful" communication.

WANT TO BE SUCCESSFUL SOCIALLY? LEARN TO LISTEN!

When we set out to change our behaviour or our thinking patterns, there is a pressure that we often place on ourselves. This pressure can hinder the change process and wear us out before we reach our goal. So often with change, there emerges what is known as the *Principle of Paradox*: "The harder you try to change, the less you succeed!" Therefore, we require a diversion that will enable us to remove the pressure and allow the change process to unfold at its own pace.

I remember one client who had been working so hard to change. He wanted people to get close to him, but he was also afraid of that closeness. Afraid that people would come on too strong or become overbearing. Afraid that he would not be able to control his feelings and that they would take over his life, as had happened in the past. Afraid that he would give up his personal power and completely defer to the other person's needs and wants. Afraid that he would end up feeling empty and angry at himself.

We hit a plateau in therapy when these fears surfaced and he just wanted to climb back into his shell. He wanted to be alone and not have to worry about relationships and "doing it right". I decided to do a 180-degree change in therapeutic direction.

"Let's take the heat off you," I began. "Stop trying to change! Instead focus on being …." Ah! Mmm! I had many options to choose from, but finally blurted out "… a *better listener*. Begin to see yourself as a really good active listener." I passed on the theory of how to be a better listener, along with some specific instructions. Instead of trying to get closer to people, just listen to them.

A couple of weeks later, he reported back that by focusing on others, on really listening to their lives and issues and not to his own fears, he actually felt more comfortable in their presence and became much less fearful.

"Do something different—listen better" is all he needed to hear to spin him into action. The inertia was changed from "I can't, I never have been successful with people before" to "I don't have to do anything, just listen, no pressure" and things changed on their own!

**Sometimes the best strategy is
"Change first, and worry about the direction later."**

"NOT ACCEPTED" IS PREFERABLE TO "BEING REJECTED"

In North America, there is an interesting quirk that sometimes arises in our choice of language. The anomaly is that we often find it easier to describe what we don't have or don't feel, rather than what we do. It seems that we start from the negative and work our way forward from there.

> *"How are you?"*
> "Not bad!"
> *"How is your job?"*
> "I haven't been fired!"
> *"How is your relationship going?"*
> "She hasn't left me yet!"

My client, a talented young professional, shared how devastated he was when his relationship ended and how totally rejected he felt. I listened compassionately, wondering how I could be helpful in his grief. He described his ex-partner in terms that were less than glowing. And at one point, he admitted that she had many characteristics and traits that he found unacceptable. He began talking himself into the "fact" that it was probably a good thing that they broke up, but he still felt rejected and hurt.

I heard myself saying—and here comes the reframe—"You know, I don't think you were as much *rejected* by this person as you were deemed *unacceptable* by her." He was very curious where this was going. Me, too! "What do you mean?" he inquired. As I stalled for time, a prolonged "Wellllllll" rolled off my tongue, and I repeated my initial thought:

> *The way I see it, you weren't as much let go or rejected as you were judged by her to be "unacceptable". And since you know that you weren't able to fulfill the needs of this person whom you have identified as being arrogant and self-centred,*

> *then maybe it's alright not to be acceptable to such a person. In fact, thank goodness you are not acceptable! Because not being acceptable to such a person speaks positive volumes about who you are!*

Based on the enormous smile that slowly crept across his lips, I thought he was going to bounce out of his chair and "high five" me on the spot. This *reframing* really works!

If we have the option—and we do—then let's decide that being judged to be unacceptable by an unacceptable person is quite acceptable, and does not constitute a rejection, but a relief.

YOU HAVE TO LISTEN IF YOU ARE GOING TO HEAR ANYTHING!

She and I had spent several previous sessions working on *communication skills*. Her husband had decided it was not necessary to attend any of the counselling sessions because "she" was the problem. She had decided that whether or not he attended, she was going to work on her communication skills. Her hope was that if she communicated differently with him, he might be motivated to change and develop more of a relationship with his kids and with her.

She reported at the next session that she had been making a lot of assertive "I" statements in conversation with her husband. She felt good about that, but the protracted anger she felt toward him hadn't really dissipated, and that really concerned her.

She shared her disappointments with him, particularly at his not being available to take over the responsibility of their children on a multitude of occasions when she had to work; instead, she had to find a babysitter. She calmly shared her feelings with him and didn't dump on him. Not bad for her first month of using the new "I" language!

At our next session, she revealed it had been a bad two weeks. She had shared with him, using "I" language, "… how disappointed I am about …", but he felt that he was being blamed for her disappointment and launched into a defence of his behaviour. His response could have been because she still had some tone, inflection or body posture issues that were being communicated as blame, or his ears were still hearing blame that was no longer there. To her credit, she worked hard to not respond or react to this defensiveness.[23]

Most often, it is not the precipitating event that does the most damage to a relationship—being late for supper, forgetting a birthday, not phoning when late, or, in this case, not taking responsibility for the kids. It is the

---

[23] Rosin, *Finding Balance*, p. 53.

lack of acknowledgement of the person's feelings about that event that does the real damage.

If the listener—in this case the husband— continues to defend himself and doesn't listen and acknowledge the feelings of the speaker— wife— about the "event", she is likely to feel disappointed and angry, and her bad feelings will escalate. She will be more angry and upset that her feelings about the event are not being heard rather than the actual event itself. The listener thinks the anger is because of the event and doesn't realize that he hasn't acknowledged her feelings about the event.

Males, please read the above paragraph again slowly.

And then read it again, even more slowly!

Original Precipitating Event:

1. He is perceived as not taking enough responsibility for the kids.
2. She starts sharing about how she feels:
   "I am disappointed …"
   "I am hurt that you …"
3. She expects to be listened to, but instead gets his *Defensive Position* that doesn't acknowledge her feelings about the "original event". Instead, the listener has shifted the emphasis from her feelings to his defensive position. The speaker perceives this shift as, "He doesn't care about me or my feelings."

The speaker is not listened to and feels upset about being ignored and discounted. She is no longer angry about the *original event*, but is angry about *not being listened to*.

If he knew about—and practised!—the skills of *active listening*[24], she probably would have expressed her feelings about the original event without blaming. She would have appreciated his listening, and that would have been that!

Stop Defending and Start Listening!

---

[24] Rosin, *Finding Balance*, p. 47.

STOPPERS—ANGER AND HURT

Their coping strategy was to spend little time together. If one partner did make time, the other seemed to be too busy, or in some way judged the other's effort. As a result, the partner who had reached out became frustrated and/or angry.

In an effort to preserve the relationship, and be somewhat safe while living together under the same roof, the partners unconsciously, and sometimes consciously, invested in their children whatever energy and time they had left after a busy workday. Eventually, their communication came to resemble the following pattern:

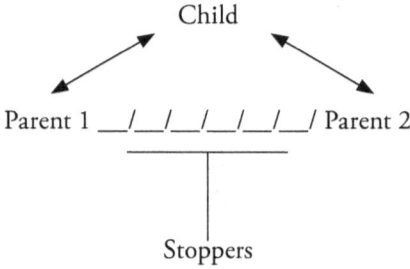

What little communication there was between the parents was constantly interrupted by what I call *Communication Stoppers*—hurtful, judgemental and disrespectful comments. Stoppers are like speed bumps, interrupting the natural flow so that partners eventually give up on each other, divert their energy into their children, and their own relationship shrivels from lack of attention.

Parents/partners often don't even realize they are starving their relationship. In fact, they often think they are being "good and concerned" parents by focusing so much on their children. While it is true that children need to feel the concern of their parents, it is equally true that adult relationships require nurturing as well. Anything less and the relationship will shrivel and may eventually die.

Children require *healthy and consistent boundaries,* which are weakened by the simultaneous lack of communication and/or the "nurturing competition" between the two parents. Consistency from both parents is a great way to convey the "boundary" messages that children need if they are to be properly guided to appropriate choices. Consistency can be best maintained through effective communication—parent–parent and parent–child.

The old scenario of the mom who says "No" and the dad who responds "Sure!" is a prime example of what I am referring to. It is a big mistake for parents to side with a child against the other parent. It is also unwise to sabotage the other parent's relationship with their child by getting into power struggles with them and countermanding their authority—put downs, belittling, sarcasm.

A commitment to reach across that person–person gap takes courage. It takes a conscious decision to share powerful and private feelings with one another. In some cases, these feelings are such that both individuals have spent a lifetime practising how to keep them contained or restrained. The ability to talk about one's anger, hurt and disappointment without blaming by using "I" language, is difficult yet imperative to the process of open and honest communication.

It is through the parent–parent relationship
that all else flows in a family!
Work on it! Protect it! Cherish it!

MAYBE IT'S OKAY TO BE A LITTLE CRAZY?

We had spent many hours together examining his poor relationships with his parents, partners and friends, and the many other issues he shared. He was always looking for a specific reason for "why" the problem happened and then sought earnestly for a "one solution" answer to the problem. When he couldn't logically find one, it was not beyond him to make one up. Our conversation began when he stated in a very dramatic voice,

"I think I have OCD! What can I do about it?"

"What have you done up to now that leads you to believe you have Obsessive Compulsive Disorder (OCD)?"

"I keep checking the doors and stove, and I wash my hands several times a day. I am really getting upset!"

"So it's getting in your way, taking up too much time? I happen to think that checking the doors and stove and keeping one's hands clean is a good thing. As you have described it, the frequency with which you do these things is not really that excessive. I do not think there is anything inherently wrong with your behaviours, but if you feel there is a problem …."

"No, it's not getting in my way, but (in an agitated voice) I am beginning to think that I am crazy. I shouldn't be like this!"

We discussed his symptoms further and how he had been coping with them. I carefully gauged the seriousness of his "OCD" statement against his recurring history of applying "a flavour of the month" diagnosis to all his problems. I believed this most recent diagnosis was simply "attention grabbing behaviour" originating from personality and not psychological issues. I therefore attempted to reframe what he had shared with me.

"Maybe it's okay to be a little bit crazy. It could make life less boring, maybe even exciting!" I wanted him to change his perspective from his view that "I am crazy and this is bad" to perhaps "I am a little bit eccentric and this could add a little bit of excitement to my life!"*

My observations began to sink in and his face lit up. I knew that he was thinking, "Yeah! Maybe this could be okay!" I continued. "So let's be clear concerning these repetitive behaviours—doors, stove, hands. They could be problematic if you did them more than three times in a row. However, anything less than three times is considered prudent and normal."

I was making this entire assessment up as I went along, and although he seemed to know that, all the while his face was steadily showing greater relief. Feeling no need to apologize for my "less than serious" approach, I kept up the game behind a scholarly doctor's face and tone. "Your homework is to repeat the behaviour in question two times and then stop! Two times is the new 'appropriate normal'. Anything more than twice would be considered problematic and not acceptable, right?"

---

*   Please don't see my method of dealing with this issue as a proper or an acceptable way of dealing with the very serious medical condition -OCD. In this example I never believed for a moment that the person (s) had the condition; if I had believed it, I certainly would have opted for a different treatment method or referred to a specialist. I present this case merely to show that, when in therapy with people who tends to shift their search outside of self for the root of their problems, it might be helpful to reframe the condition and play with it a bit. In this example I encouraged the person (s) to continue their symptoms under limited circumstances (until they no longer needed them) and to see self as a "normal but eccentric person", a role they relished.

"Right!" he responded, with a glow and a smile.

I was amazed that he accepted this "new normal" so readily. If I had told him to stop his behaviour altogether—door, stove, hands—he probably would have become upset. When I told him to do only so much of the behaviour, he was a lot happier. Interesting!

Reframing and reducing (even slightly) compulsive behaviours and inferring they are within the "normal" range, certainly is more hopeful than a "sick or crazy" label.

TALK TO ME!

In order for couples to improve their communication, you have to provide clear directions for them on how to get there. The standard therapeutic tool of "Okay, your homework is to meet each day at 10:00 pm— kids finally in bed and after an exhausting day—and then talk to each other." No, that will not work. All you will get are some classic "go-nowhere" replies—"Yep! Nope! Nothing! Okay!"—that will lead fairly quickly to a strained silence.

I have found that people often do a lot of intellectual thinking and planning with clear expectations for their partner, but they don't necessarily share those thoughts with them. What I suggest is that couples create a daily routine where they take the time to go through a series of questions at an appropriate time—at the supper table.

By asking and answering these questions, they will at least attend to the many expectations they have for each other, while sharing and communicating with one another. Start with the mundane details of your day and end up by sharing your feelings.

Questions to ask your partner daily:

How was your day?

What are you thinking about that needs doing tonight/tomorrow?

How can we help each other?

What happened in your day that we both need to know about—particularly to do with kids, family, friends and neighbours?

What expectations do you have for me this evening? Over the next 24 hours?[25]

**If it is answers that you seek,
you'd best know the right questions!**

---

[25] David Waters, The Big Moment, *Psychotherapy Networker,* Nov/Dec 2005, p. 38.

SUCCESSFUL CHANGE REQUIRES CONSCIOUSNESS, FOCUS AND REPETITION

Changing one's self—how one thinks, feels, values or believes—can be very difficult to do. It can be even more difficult to maintain.

While sometimes desirable, an individual's ability to work toward "change" can feel extremely uncomfortable. It is much like forcing a right-handed person to use only their left hand. At the first sign of frustration or stress, the changes that have been made will likely be abandoned, and the individual will revert back to old, familiar ways of doing things.

To be successful at *changing ourselves*—from being an angry person to being a calm one, or from being a self-centred person to one who really listens to others—we must remain highly motivated. To change, one requires a new vision of what things will look like after the changes have been instituted.

Change most often occurs under the following circumstances— when we feel *safe*; when the changes result in something *better* than what we currently have; when we realize that we can manage or *accept* the reactions of others to these changes; and when our *self-esteem* is high enough to overcome our fears of taking risks through change, of the potential for failure, or of embarrassment.

Maintaining what we have changed requires that we remain *conscious* and *focused* on our goals. It requires many repetitions of the new behaviours—doing the new behaviours *on purpose* and *repeatedly*—if change is to be permanent.

> **If you're serious about changing your behaviour, make a contract with the significant people in your life to help you monitor your progress!**

YOU NEED TO FEEL SAFE TO CHANGE

I have often found that people consider making changes in their lives when they reach the "end of their rope", when they feel that they can't go any lower than they have already gone, or when they feel *safe*. Safe, in that they don't feel pressured, threatened or intimidated to change. They are confident they can respond, and satisfied that they can handle whatever is presented to them.

When people choose to make changes that result in them taking better care of themselves instead of tending to every need of their family, friends or colleagues, these former recipients of that exclusive care generally resent the personal changes that are being made. They can often become upset that you are being so selfish by taking care of your needs over theirs. They would prefer you stay the same, continue to look after their needs, and remain predictable. This familiarity in how you look, feel, think and act provides them—and, to a degree, you—with a level of comfort.

Inherent in change, however, is the unknown—"How will I (or others) respond to the changes?"

"What is appropriate?"

"What will people think?"

"How will they judge me?"

"Can I handle it?"

"Is it worth the effort?" There is a period when your confidence needs to carry you until the people in your life realize that your changes will add more to their lives as well.

People mostly change when they feel safe and have the confidence to do so. Change brought about by intimidation is seldom permanent, lasting only about as long as the threat is present. The one who feels threatened will most often quickly revert back to their old ways once the pressure has been removed.

If you feel safe in a relationship or in a period of your life, and if you are confident that some contemplated changes are right for you, and if you can muster the courage to begin the process to enact this change even though you know that not everyone you care about will appreciate the changes, you will not only have a changed lifestyle, but vastly improved self-esteem as well.

> *When contemplating change, don't make the big announcement, the big speech about what you're going to do. Just do it! As the old adage goes, "Actions speak louder than words!"*

A positive change in lifestyle can lead to an improved self-esteem.

CHANGE IS ABOUT OPTIONS

I believe that we need:
- *to learn to not take ourselves so seriously.*
- *to learn to love who we are, instead of finding other people's qualities so appealing. Abandon those thoughts that if I were only taller, smaller, lighter, heavier, smarter, funnier, then I would be okay.*
- *to start giving ourselves strokes for what we actually do and who we are, and make that enough!*
- *to learn to laugh at ourselves.*

We cannot eradicate our past. We cannot ignore that we held, and still hold, habits and beliefs that we acquired early in our lives, which have led to the behaviours that define who we are today. We need to accept ourselves, particularly if we want other people to accept us. We need to accept that we have some "crazy parts" that need changing and not be defensive about those changes. We need to realize that we need more support than criticism if we are to bring about the desired changes.

When we recognize and take ownership of our "crazy parts", then we become open to other possibilities. The energy that we so needlessly wasted on denying or controlling ourselves so that others won't find out about our "unacceptable parts", or so that they won't discover "who we really are", is then redirected and invested in those enriching *projects of change* that enable us to live life more fully.

Acknowledging that change is possible—not easy, but possible—is recognizing that we have more options than we thought. We now need to find the courage to explore what these options are and choose what is best for us in the present!

Work at changing your crazy parts that are not useful or appropriate, but don't feel bad about them!

WE ARE BOTH DOING GOOD WORK!

He was really feeling down. He thought that all of the issues he had "overcome" while in therapy were behind him. But here he was, feeling those same old feelings once again and wondering if he had really changed at all. He was still feeling as though he did not belong, that people did not like him, and that no one cared. He was in pain and yet, quite inadvertently, he was still doing everything he possibly could to push people away with his abrasive, cold and "know-it-all" behaviours. All his life he felt that he was not good enough. It didn't matter how hard he tried or how successful he was, the feeling always remained the same: "They wouldn't like me if they really knew me." He created a scar that would not heal.

He was greatly disappointed in "having done the work" and now feeling that nothing had changed. His lack of hope and despair showed in his eyes. I let him voice his feelings aloud. He painted a picture of deep sadness and loneliness. Finally, I stopped him as he began repeating his negative feelings.

I wanted to share a different view and pointed out that the things he was describing to me were not all as *hopeless and helpless* as he made them out to be. Yes, he had temporarily lost his way and his focus on living *life differently*. And yes, at this moment he had reverted back to old familiar feelings and patterns. But I had seen many changes in him over the last year and he seemed to have forgotten all of the good things that he had been doing.

I cited a few positive examples that demonstrated some of his breakthroughs and achievements. Some of the evidence that he needed to appreciate that he *had* been doing things differently. He looked confused and persisted in his negativity. I asked him to think about the ways that he had successfully changed and who might have noticed those changes.

At first, he seemed absolutely committed to being down on himself for his "failures". But after a few minutes, he begrudgingly volunteered a few examples of how he had reached out to others, and how people had in turn responded to him very positively. Throughout this, he was trying awfully hard to stick to his familiar refrain that "I am an awful person and nobody likes me."

So there he was, providing me with examples of how he was treating people differently, responding more positively and being more open to them. Yet at the same time, he was also declaring— almost using the voice of a hurt little boy—that he had not changed and all of his hard work was for naught. "I might as well just plan to be alone and stay away from people. At least I wouldn't get so hurt," he concluded. *As if being alone and lonely didn't hurt!*

I didn't reply and allowed his self-pitying rant to run its course. I wasn't about to give his "poor me" attitude any further attention. His tone not only implied that he had failed, but also seemed to indicate that as his therapist, I had failed him as well. His anger and self-loathing finally came to an end and he tentatively asked, in his little boy's voice, "Do you think I have changed?" Now I knew he was ready to hear me.

"Yes!" I enthusiastically asserted. "You are doing good work, and even though on some days you don't feel different or better, your actual behaviour indicates that you are making great progress. The work you have done is making a difference; just hang in there." Indeed, he hung on to every word as though it were a life preserver.

Occasionally, I have to remind myself that being helpful isn't always about what *I do* or about my ability to apply miraculous insights or techniques. Sometimes it's as simple as believing in the client's ability to make their world better. Supporting them in their efforts and reminding them that they are on track. I have found that this is often more than enough to constitute the help that they need. Like this person, I sometimes place too much pressure on myself to effect positive results!

How does that famous intervention from the Single Session Therapeutic School of Inappropriate Therapy go? Slap! Just Stop It!

THE BEST PREDICTOR...

How many performances do you need to see before you can decide if you like the play?

The client kept giving her partner another chance. He was prone to over-indulging in alcohol and she recently caught him with another woman.

What was clear to me was that he wasn't going to change because he kept denying his behaviour was a problem. He would buy her off with a few weeks of "good behaviour" and attentiveness, and then, as their history showed, he would repeat the cycle (alcohol and women).

I shared with her the saying, "The best predictor of tomorrow's weather is today's", hoping she would hear the imbedded message. I wasn't saying that he *couldn't* change; only that it seemed to me that he wasn't *planning* to change because he didn't perceive his behaviour as a problem. Or maybe he didn't take responsibility for his behaviour because there were no real consequences—she always took him back.

She decided that giving him more chances was just putting off the inevitable, which she stated was no longer an option for her. However, because she had low self-esteem, she was afraid to be alone and fearful that she wouldn't find anything better. So she kept the relationship alive.

She certainly didn't need to see the play again to know the ending, and yet she continued to hope it would turn out differently. I suggested that her "hope" sounded like the pop definition of insanity—"doing the same thing over and over and hoping for a different outcome".

Eventually, the pain of this relationship will be greater than her fear of being alone and she will find the courage to end it. Unfortunately, for this couple, I believed there were still several years of "cycling" before that would occur.

Being "concerned" has an action component that could lead to change. Worry goes nowhere.

The best predictor of tomorrow's weather— and behaviour—is today's!

THAT'S A CHOICE, NOT A CONDITION

The client presented himself as cool, perhaps even sullen and aloof. There was no spark in his eyes and no joy in his life. He said he had always been that way and he was content. 'Then why are you in my office?' I thought quietly to myself.

His self-styled description of his life—"this is the way I have always been"—sounded to me like an excuse and, at best, a mask for his rigid behaviour and unfulfilling lifestyle. My response to this description of his life was, "Being the way you have always been is a choice, not a condition." Surprisingly, this simple statement seemed to give him permission to consider a change in how he lived his life. It had never occurred to him that lifestyle was a choice.

In our youth, when we have no personal power, lack wisdom and are still developing our rational thinking on how our behaviour affects us and others, it is often justifiable to plead, "I did my best" or "This is who I am." However, as an adult with power, and the ability to shape our behaviours and lifestyles, it is not appropriate to repeat the debilitating refrain, "That's the way I have been and that's the way I'll stay." *Changing isn't easy, but it is an option.*

Choose your behaviour, choose to get more out of life, choose to be more fulfilled. Choose a more gratifying job, or choose to make your relationship better. Choose to see value in every person you meet. Think differently and throw away some of your old rules. Relax. And, despite your upbringing, have some fun. You really do have a choice!

Change starts with *minute change* in the *now*. So, just get started!

**Changing or "staying the same"
is a choice, not a condition.**

UNDERSTANDABLE, BUT NO LONGER APPROPRIATE

A saying I use quite often is, "It's understandable, but no longer appropriate." This means that many of the ways you learned to adapt and keep yourself safe in childhood and adolescence need no longer be acceptable now that you are an adult.

Don't beat yourself up if you still use these antiquated methods—crying, playing stupid, passive. Just update your methods! Find new and more powerful ways—adult and mature ways—to respond to problems, disagreements and issues. Retire the old ways and work on developing new ones, like improving communication skills; "talking" about being angry instead of "being" angry; giving up "winning" arguments and instead having "discussions".

Young people generally don't have rational thought until somewhere around ages 11 to 13, so most of their early coping strategies are devised without the benefit of this more advanced thinking process. Most teens don't like themselves much, have low self-esteem, and are still quite dependent on the adults in their lives. They are needy, but kick and scream for independence. They are extremely negative and critical toward those same adults upon whom they are dependent for food, shelter, financing, love and strokes. Interesting! Perhaps it is this dependency that has them so angry.

When we review the treatment we received as children and how we learned to cope in our family environment, we need to accept that the way we act when dealing with others as adults is quite understandable. If we still use these old coping mechanisms, and they continue to be marginally successful or are childish and embarrassing, then it is time to make a change. We need to realize that we sometimes get in our own way. We need to understand what isn't working and find new ways of replying to life's problems and issues.

**Children basically have no power
and their survival strategies reflect that absence!
Adults have power (if they choose to use it)
and their behaviours need to reflect that choice!**

TO MY PARENTS

When children are young, they have no power to "fight back" against, or to cope with, the inconsistencies, idiosyncrasies and sometimes downright crazy behaviour of the adults in their lives. As well as learning about love, it is in families that kids learn about unfairness, poor treatment, being ignored, and abuse. As a result of their negative experiences, many decide that they are "less"—less important, less loveable—than they really are. They develop low self-esteem, and often learn to *survive* rather than *live*.

When these children become adults, they in fact possess greater personal power than when they were young. However, they often continue to use the same survival mechanisms they used when they were children. They ignore their power and have remained angry with the adults from their childhood. And they often deal with the people in their present lives by using the same coping strategies from the "bad old days".

We need to realize and own the impact that our previous life had on us when, as a vulnerable child, we had little power to defend ourselves. And as an adult, we need to understand and accept that we have "new" power, and that we can create new ways of relating in the present, particularly to the "grown-ups" from our past. We also need to realize that our parents and other significant adults can no longer be given credit or blamed for how we feel or act in the present. I repeat myself:

> *I choose to have you in my life, but you aren't my life. I want you close, but I also want a life separate from you.*

I no longer need you—my parent(s)—to define who I am.

HOMEWORK FOR A VICTIM

Did you ever have to write lines at school? You were probably being punished for talking too much, chewing gum, or not doing your homework. You were punished for some indiscretion and the lines were, unfortunately, to help remind you "what not to do". I think schoolteachers nowadays would instead have you consider a positive action and write "what to do!"

In working with a victim of child abuse, she/we came up with the following list of new feelings and responsibilities that she was now ready to own. For homework, I encouraged her to read each of the following lines and add, "And that is now true for me, or truer for me than it has ever been." Doing these lines was not punishment, but validation.

- I have personal power and that gives me choices.
- I am responsible for that power.
- I am responsible for the direction of my life. I am responsible for how I interact with people.
- I believe I am powerful when I speak out. I believe I can "handle and deal with" whatever surprises the world has for me.
- I believe I will not fall apart if someone disagrees with me.
- I know my Adult (A) will provide safety for my Child (C).[26]
- I love my (C). She is creative and fun-loving and definitely a survivor. I have changed and there are many more good things still to come.

The privilege of seeing someone believe they can now "handle" and be responsible for their life is very gratifying.

If you don't like the story of your life, rewrite it with a different ending!

---

[26] Rosin, *Finding Balance*, p. 141.

EGO

A female client stated, "I didn't think women had much of an *ego*, but I am beginning to change my mind!"

My response to this was, "Sometimes it is important to have a healthy ego to remind us to take care of ourselves—whether it's practising good hygiene, dressing appropriately, painting our house, or finding the drive to receive good marks in school." My client didn't particularly view ego as a good thing.

To be sure, there is a less than positive side to ego—when women, and to a higher degree men, play *fun* sports beyond fun to where it becomes one big competition and they no longer enjoy doing it; when they drive themselves so hard just to show their friends how good or powerful they are, even if their health is detrimentally affected; when they start a war just to prove they can't be pushed around; when they get a facelift; or when they need "much younger than themselves" relationships!

Although it probably is never correct to assume anything, I assume that both men and women require a healthy ego. In the right context and within measure, it can help them take better care of and feel better about themselves. Remember:

> *Nobody needs an inflated ego—you are who you are. You are not a "Jones", so there is no need to keep up with them!*

Feeling "pleased and proud" is the result of a healthy ego. Being "arrogant and conceited" is the result of an inflated ego.

NEEDY!

In humans, the degree of their *need* is often proportionate to the level of their *self-esteem*.

Low self-esteem often causes us to have *blind spots* in how we treat our partners. We focus on our flaws and are very self-critical. We become so absorbed in ourselves, in how we are repeatedly *screwing up*, that we close off and are no longer able to provide for our partner's needs.

When we have an empty *pot*[27] that requires constant attention and filling, we are not available to our partner. We are not able to fill their *pot*. And eventually, given that most relationships are reciprocal, it may well be that one day our partner will not be available for us. Low self-esteem does not allow for a great deal of generosity toward others, and in a relationship, that can be costly.

Being needy and feeling poorly about one's self is an obstacle to confronting our partner on what they are doing—drinking, playing around, finances—or not doing—caring about us, the kids, finances. Sometimes, it's not an absence of concern that takes away our motivation from confronting inappropriate behaviour, but rather the fear of confronting the other person because they might leave us. So, we often choose to live with *crumbs*, instead of insisting on eating from the fullness of the whole pie.

When our self-esteem has been low for some time, we almost expect things to go wrong, and they generally do. We learn to settle for very little *from* our relationships. And in turn, we give very little *to* our relationships.

I believe almost everyone has issues with self-esteem in their lives. And if they are to be successful at reversing this "down" position and improving their self-esteem, they need to have a plan—give more strokes to self, stay focused and be consistent with their strokes to self.

Low self-esteem is not a life sentence—get help!

---

[27] Rosin, *Communication & Relationships*, p. 107.

LIGHT YOUR LAMP

My client was just leaving after an hour's session that focused on her flagging relationship. As I walked her to the door, I felt compelled to say:

> *If you need another person to light your lamp—to make you feel good about yourself—and your light doesn't come from inside of you, then you have given your personal power away. The other person will realize what you have done and will either abuse you, leave you, or most assuredly have no respect for you.*

She looked at me like she had been hit with a ton of bricks, and then thanked me!

In the past, she had ended many relationships "before they did." Now she was contemplating her current relationship, where she felt cared for but didn't believe it would last. She thought perhaps it was time to end it.

It seemed to me that the outcomes of her relationships always followed the same two patterns—either *she felt cared for* by someone but didn't believe that this caring relationship would last and so she ended it, or *she did not feel cared for*, worked harder at making the relationship work, and ended up feeling angry with the other person for having treated her poorly. She also felt angry with herself for putting up with the poor treatment.

She repeatedly created a destructive, "no win" cycle through these patterns, such that her self-esteem was so low that she did not see herself as a worthy person. She was afraid of being hurt and believed that "it was her fate to be treated badly". And so, she was getting ready to run, again.

What I said to her at the door about lighting her own lamp seemed to resonate. When you start loving yourself, and you are "in charge" of taking care of yourself, then you will stop being so dependent on others, stop being so afraid of being hurt, and learn to love someone else. You will then have the confidence to know you can handle whatever arises— be it positive or negative—and not have to run away.

**Be "in charge" of your own self-esteem.
Light your own candle.**

UPDATE AND UPGRADE!

The Child (C) doesn't easily forget the lessons of infancy and adolescence, lessons that are often forged out of the necessity to survive.

Rational Thinking and Personal Power are very important attributes for good decision-making. Yet, they don't develop until somewhere between ages 11 and 13 or even later. Children are often forced into making *life decisions* long before they possess the necessary tools to do so. As a result, they often make bad decisions and are stuck with feelings of inadequacy for all time.

Maybe I am jaded, but I see almost every personal problem coming back to the issue of self-esteem. Dramatic? Perhaps, but low self-esteem seems to be a precipitating factor in most problematic adult behaviours.

I believe these early decisions that a child makes are completely understandable—the best a 3, 6, or 9 year old with limited resources can make at that time. Unfortunately, the decisions they are forced to make centre around surviving in a dysfunctional family or community that is primarily made up of critical, often violent adults with low self-esteem who just don't make the time or possess the understanding to connect with their children.

Sadly, these "role models" dole out many more negative strokes than positive nurturing strokes to their children, which leaves scars that often lead to destructive behaviours.

When I see these children as adults, they are often quite convinced that how they feel about themselves, or how they have learned to act— their behaviour—is set in stone. They are convinced that this is who they are. They do not easily let new data in that would paint a different picture of them than the one they've carried since childhood.

As adults, the criterion that we use to judge how we feel about ourselves needs to be updated. It can no longer be based on our antiquated childhood feelings. The Adult (A) needs to establish this upgraded criterion based on who the person is *today*.

Often the old feelings that are harboured by the Child (C) completely prevent my clients from seeing who they now are as adults. Some see themselves as warm and loving individuals who others want to be near, but at the same time, feel inadequate and confused about why anyone would want to be close to them. It is not easy to like yourself when you haven't done so for most of your life. It is not easy to practise self-care when you have never felt worthwhile.

People with low self-esteem need to start identifying and counting all the good things they *do* and *are* on a daily basis. They need to realize that an original decision made as a kid that "I am not okay" was premature. They need to redecide that they are okay based on who they are now and the rational information they now have as adults.

"I am okay" is an upgrade based on current information.

FOUR PATHS OF LOW SELF-ESTEEM

When a person has been convinced early in their life that they are not capable, not clever, and are continuously discounted, it results in a feeling of low self-esteem, and they either withdraw into themselves or defer to others.

In some cases, however, they decide on a third option—that how they see things is absolutely correct. They lose all objectivity. In fact, they become quite antagonistic if challenged or presented with a different perspective. They are convinced they are right and are "sick and tired of being told I am wrong". They are angry, put "all my eggs in this one basket", and go to war on every issue. It's a fight to the finish with everything.

Low self-esteem can lead down one of several divergent and inappropriate paths. One path is where we do not have the confidence to speak up and declare our truth. Another path is believing virtually everybody says it better and is cleverer than they are. The third path is one of "if you want to know the right answer, just ask me". This person knows everything about everything and they are always right.

There is also a fourth path symbolized by the saying, "I am okay—you are okay." We break the cycle by learning to love ourselves and respect others.

Despite being born into a family that discourages the building of positive self-esteem, we can still break the cycle!

WATCH YOUR LANGUAGE

When he returned to my office, I recalled that we had talked a year before about his broken relationship. This time he "dropped by" to see me because he felt as though his behaviour at work was being perceived as *inappropriate*.

Nobody had informed him it was, but it was his nature to over analyze and think the worst. He was so serious and hard on himself and could not let minor confrontations just be. He had to build them into a "big deal". He felt he was getting into the habit of *overreacting* and people were getting tired of telling him not to worry. They were exhausted from trying to show him that the issue he was "going off on" was really nothing. It seemed that even the most benign remark about his behaviour or work caused him hours of self-recrimination. His colleagues were getting sick of reassuring him!

Over and over again, he referred to himself as a *screw up*. He didn't see himself as an ordinary person who made the occasional mistake. He *was* the mistake. As evidenced by the language he used to refer to himself, it seemed that in his mind he was a living, breathing example of a person who always screws up. "I don't just screw up, I *am* a screw up," he constantly repeated. His language on this subject was resolute, and it pronounced him guilty in all possible instances. It was a self-imposed life sentence. He believed he was a screw up, and therefore he was.

He grew mildly curious when I mentioned that I believed that "Healthy, average people screw up. We all make mistakes and this is considered normal." In hindsight, it was like going after a battleship with a BB gun! He conceded that making mistakes was normal for others, but for himself, it was a screw up bordering on personal failure.

He shared that at a very vulnerable moment as a youngster, he had it impressed on him by a significant adult that he was "useless and a screw up". Unfortunately, it stuck. As an adolescent, he was not a good athlete and did not excel in school. As an adult, he ended up working in low paying jobs with little satisfaction. His marriage had failed. He learned to discount himself as a way of putting himself down before others had the opportunity to do so. *Beat them to the punch*, was his motto.

We had a lot of work to do, but unfortunately he didn't have the desire or the belief that he could change to do it!

I am always a little bothered when I cannot or do not get the chance to be helpful. Maybe it's my competitive nature, or that I just get upset when people give up because they have been "gotten to" early in their lives and see no options for themselves. My client believed what *was* now *is forever*. It was engraved in his mind and etched into his every thought. Unfortunately, his behaviour would always reflect his belief that he was a screw up. Three sessions later and I was fired!

I think, therefore I am!

WRITE, SHARE, BURY AND BURN!

I find that people often beat themselves up on a regular basis by recycling old thoughts and feelings about things that they have done or what people have done to them that are less than ideal. Things they feel embarrassed about. Behaviours they wish they hadn't engaged in, past indiscretions and wrong doings. It's all part of a history that they would be better off forgetting. The problem is they don't!

We forgive others so much more easily than we forgive ourselves. We carry around a garbage bag that never gets emptied, only added to. Every once in a while—and some people do this daily—we take out the contents and smack ourselves around a bit by asking why we did what we did in the past. Even if something occurred in a different part of our life, we still don't cut ourselves any slack.

We need to forgive, let go and move on! If we don't, it is almost guaranteed that we will become or remain an angry person with low self-esteem. In order to find peace, we need to focus on our successes, not on our "screw ups".

What I encourage my clients to do when they are stuck in these games of "Ain't it awful that …", "I can't move on until they …" or "I can't change until I am forgiven by …", is to do some therapeutic writing.

I introduce it this way. "You seem to have a number of significant events and experiences in your life that continue to have a negative impact on you. I encourage you to identify those events and write about them."

If one of the negative experiences is a relationship, I may ask them to write about what was *good* and *not so good* about the relationship, and *what could have been* if they had stayed together.[28]

I encourage my clients to take the time and invest the energy in surfacing these bits of their past, to write about them, and then return and explain to me the significance of these events in their life. The key is

---

[28] Rosin, *Finding Balance*, p. 78.

that I am asking them to explain the significance of these events for the last time. And yes, I am planting the *for the last time seed* in their thinking.

I take time and listen to their stories. Then I suggest symbolic ways that can be practised to end my clients' tendency to recycle these negative memories. I introduce them to visualization—have them picture these past events being buried in solid steel safes, underground, or in 400 feet of water. Sometimes even encased in kryptonite or on board a lunar spaceship bound for Mars!

It is the brain that conjures up the past and it is the brain that needs to find safe and *out-of-reach* places to bury these memories so they are not easily accessible. In effect, we need to *trick* the brain into having to choose to work extremely hard to access these negative memories from the past so that it won't access them again.

There are enough people and events in our *present* life to compromise our self-esteem. We don't have to go into our past to come up with examples to feel bad. Let go of all that old negative stuff and just concentrate on making good choices, in the *Now!* In that way, we will lead ourselves to who we want to be and the kind of lifestyle we want.

"Let go" (of the past) and "let live" (in the now).

STROKE POT

Stories get told and embellished with time. They get retold in ways that suit the teller. This can be done to make a point clearer or to introduce more drama. I am certainly glad I don't do that!

At this point, I can see my adult children rolling their eyes!

A story I have told for many years to introduce the concept of strokes originated with Virginia Satir.

Virginia Satir was a family therapist, workshop facilitator, and celebrated author.[29] As I tell it, Virginia's story—which may be folklore—focuses on her life growing up on a farm during the "Dirty Thirties" and how this helped her understand what starvation felt like. Her experience later helped her create the concept of strokes and what happens to people when they don't receive enough of them.

As the story goes, the land was in drought, crops had failed and food was very scarce. There was a big pot on the stove in the kitchen. If you looked in it and there was food, your spirits were raised because it meant you were going to eat that day. If there was nothing in the pot, you felt down.

Years later, she remembered these "up" and "down" days with the crock pot and coined the term *pot*—as a kind of storage vessel—along with the term *strokes*. As she described them, these strokes were *units of recognition, compliments, caring touch*. Virginia envisioned each person as having a *stroke pot* inside themselves. When it is filled, they feel good and their self-esteem is high.

---

[29] Virginia Satir, *Peoplemaking,* Paulo Alto, CA, Science and Behavior Books, Inc., 1972.

After reading Virginia Satir's books and having had the great fortune to meet her twice, she made it very clear to me and all attendees at her workshops that the responsibility for filling one's own *stroke pot* rests with the individual.

> **If you wait for the world—partner, friend, job—
> to fill your pot, you will starve!
> By the way, strokes presented with laughter
> have double the value!**

EXTERNAL AND INTERNAL STROKES

The majority of people in North America grow up receiving acceptable *strokes*—units of recognition—from parents, community, school, and religious groups. These acceptable strokes are earned by being a *good little girl or boy*, receiving good grades in school, going to an acceptable college, choosing the right partner, getting a promotion, making lots of money, acquiring power, and by rescuing people and/or systems from failure.

It's a shame that more people are not taught to give themselves strokes for being healthy and pursuing quality of life!

I find that all too often, people are taught to value only the *external strokes* given by others who share their values. These values are based on the elements described above, and while they may involve a degree of personal satisfaction in terms of a sense of accomplishment or achievement, they are generally fleeting or passing pleasures that require continual accomplishment or achievement to sustain the degree of satisfaction felt.

Although much good comes from these external strokes, many are outdated and restrictive, and don't take into account individual differences, age differences, or changes in the times.

By contrast, *internal strokes* focus on achieving and leading a balanced, healthy *lifestyle* and revolve around things of lasting or permanent value. A healthy and strong physique derived from a regular exercise regimen and healthy eating habits, investments of time, wisdom and guidance in the context of family and children, and taking moments to enjoy the fruits of one's labour, are all things that provide lasting satisfaction while often leading to sustained accomplishment and achievement.

I am reminded of Abraham Maslow's[30] concept of Self Actualization, and I understate: *to be all you can be*. To self actualize is the only way to the *lasting satisfaction* I talk about in the previous paragraph. I say "be all you can be, and then stroke the hell out of yourself for doing what you

---

[30] Abraham Maslow, *The Further Reachers of Human Nature,* New York, NY, Arkana: Penguin Books, 1993.

have done". Maslow would say that only through self-actualization can one fulfill the deepest longing of one's being.

Therefore, if we are to be healthy and *in balance*, we need both *external strokes*—from others—that reflect societal values, as well as *internal strokes*—from self—that reward individual differences and self-nourishment.

If we don't stroke ourselves, there is a good chance we will go through life in a stroke-deprived state[31] with a whack of behaviours that reflect poor self-esteem. This is neither pretty nor very functional.

**Find a way to give yourself strokes—
or you will have to function in a stroke-deprived state!**

---

[31] Rosin, *Finding Balance,* p. 100.

STROKES AND STATESPERSONS

We don't want "others" in charge of our daily stroke levels because this leaves us at their mercy when it comes to receiving the necessary strokes we need to be healthy.[32] It seems that these "other people" only stroke us when we act appropriately (from their perspective), but then cut us off—and sometimes cast us off—when we don't meet their needs. At these times, it is important for us to understand and accept that we have no power over other people. We can't really make them like us, love us and stroke us, so we need to be prepared to do more of that for ourselves.[33]

What we can do is become more vocal and be a "statesperson", and give ourselves stokes for stating our thoughts, feelings, values and beliefs.[34] When we give ourselves strokes, we are "in-charge" of the quantity and quality of strokes we receive. If we depend too much on others for a healthy level of strokes, we will probably starve.

The need for strokes is an overwhelming drive that goes back to infancy. To a child, being rejected and cut off from parental interaction and strokes is literally a life and death matter. Adults see strokes as indicators of acceptance and worthiness—"few" strokes are experienced as rejection; "too few strokes" can diminish our self-esteem. And so we need to accept the responsibility for maintaining a healthy level of strokes for ourselves.

A statesperson is one who states their principles—what they think, feel, value and believe—and then gives themselves strokes for having the courage to state those same principles. This puts the responsibility for getting a healthy amount of strokes on to self, which means less dependency on others and more "in charge" of one's own stroke needs.

---

[32] Rosin, *Finding Balance* p. 94.
[33] Rosin, *Finding Balance* p. 102.
[34] Rosin, *Finding Balance* p. 53.

A good supply of quality strokes = high self-esteem.

**"I can't make you do anything,
but you can't shut me up (statesperson)."**

(An all-time favourite saying of mine)

STROKES AS A MATHEMATICAL FORMULA

In the course of my day, I often find myself repeating, "People/I need a certain number of strokes each day in order to feel fulfilled and be healthy."

I recently converted this healthy need for strokes into a pseudomathematical formula. To do so, I arbitrarily attributed a certain number of strokes to certain activities and actions— "greeting your significant other in the morning" is worth 1 stroke, and "saying 'I love you'" is worth 15 strokes, and so on. You might attribute different *stroke values* for the various activities, but they must add up to a certain quota for you to be healthy.

For example, let's suppose that *Person X* needs 50 strokes a day and fills his daily quota by giving himself strokes from the following activities:

working out	5 strokes
says hello, interacts superficially with work colleagues	4
takes some "down time"	2
treats himself to a massage	2
eats according to his plan	4
plays a team sport twice a week	6
goes to night school and completes an assignment	4
listens and is listened to by a friend	8
is in a positively significant relationship	15
Total	**50** strokes

In contrast, let's suppose that *Person Y* also needs 50 strokes a day. He has no significant person in his life and fills his daily quota this way:

working out	5 strokes
says hello, interacts superficially with work colleagues	4
takes some "down time"	2

treats himself to a massage	2
eats according to his plan	4
plays a team sport twice a week	6
goes to night school and completes an assignment	4
listens and is listened to by a friend	8
has two really good friends	10
has five acquaintances he plays poker with	5
Total	**50** strokes

I know it isn't realistic to divide behaviours into such definitive stroke values. But the intent of my message is that doing things we value and that are good for us is a way of giving ourselves the strokes we need in order to be healthy.[35] If we don't have a significant person in our lives who is a positive influence, then we need to find other activities or people—yes, they have a lesser stroke value, and yes, we need more of them—to fill the quota.

I recognize that there is a very real danger of becoming too dependent on that one significant person or career path in our life,[36] so it is probably best if we *overfill* the *stroke pot* with a variety of people and activities that can help balance out that dependency. In theory, it is probably a good idea to boost the daily quota to 65 strokes a day, in case a relationship ends or the job doesn't work out!

The most important point of this concept is not the actual math, but rather that you take care of yourself and do things that you determine as giving your life purpose, and then give yourself lots of strokes for doing them!

**Make healthy choices that allow you to be "in balance".
Then give yourself strokes for making these good choices.**

---

[35] Rosin, *Finding Balance,* p. 94.
[36] Rosin, *Finding Balance,* p. 101.

ME FIRST

The noted physician and endocrinologist Hans Selye once said, and I paraphrase, "The reason why you take care of yourself first is so you can, in turn, be healthy and take care of others." I concur! You cannot truly be healthy unless you commit to taking care of yourself first. And conversely, you cannot take proper care of others if you are not in good shape yourself.

To remain *in balance*, you must continuously be *conscious* of the choices you make in taking care of your *self*. It is very difficult to consistently arrive at a perfect balance point of others vs. self. However, once we take care of our needs, then we can look to others.

If you are self-centred and thinking only of yourself, you cannot remain "in balance". To reach this mythical point of balance, we need to prioritize our needs and make sure those needs get met. We also need to reach out to others. We need to be needed. We need to receive some strokes from others for what we do.

I emphasize "some" strokes from others because I believe we need to give ourselves the majority of the strokes needed to be healthy.[37] We feel fulfilled when our need to be needed is met. As well, there is something extremely gratifying when we can step up and be there for others. To be genuinely "helpful" and "not rescuing"[38] really fills our *pot*[39] with quality strokes.

As a person who works in the helping profession, I have observed that people's lives are happier and healthier when they achieve balance between caring for self and being available to others.

There is a special caution here, however. For the most part, I believe that all too often we have been encouraged to take care of others, our jobs and our families first, to the point where we forget about self. When we

---

[37] Rosin, *Finding Balance* p. 102.
[38] Rosin, *Finding Balance* p. 65.
[39] Rosin, *Communication & Relationships* p. 107.

forget about self, or conversely, when we concentrate too much on self, we run the risk of losing balance. We are then prone to becoming physically sick and/or emotionally burned out.

This *me first* concept has received much criticism. I believe people tend to interpret my encouragement of self first as adopting a "Me, Me, and to heck with others" attitude, when in fact what I'm saying is, "Me first and more for others later." People are not generous in sharing strokes with others—whether these strokes are attention or caring— when they themselves are starving.

Fill your own "pot" first and then share the wealth!

REACT OR RESPOND?

Respond to people. Don't react to them!.

It is my belief that the more *fatigued* we are, the less we exercise, and the less time we spend with family, friends and activities that fulfill or satisfy us, the emptier our *pot* is, and the lower our self-esteem becomes. Now, that's a mouthful!

If we allow our pot to remain depleted for too long, there is a greater chance that we will overreact to people's criticisms and self-centred behaviours—real or perceived. It seems there is a direct correlation between our self-esteem, our impulse to react, and fatigue.

If we take care of ourselves—in a holistic fashion focused on body, mind and spirit—and convert every opportunity into positive strokes, then we will feel more confident.

And if we respond to our chosen path more often, that is, be more proactive, we will react less often to the negative "curve balls" that life throws at us, and we will be healthier, more balanced, and have a higher self-esteem.[40][41][42][43]

Quite profound, very logical, and certainly worth repeating— which I have on several occasions throughout this book!

**When your fuel tank is low—fatigued,
low self-esteem—you React.
When your fuel tank is high—energized,
high self-esteem—you Respond.**

---

[40] Rosin, *Finding Balance*, p. 97.
[41] Rosin, *Finding Balance*, p. 101.
[42] Rosin, *Finding Balance*, p. 102.
[43] Rosin, *Finding Balance*, p. 103.

Promise yourself...

To be so strong that nothing can disturb your peace of mind.

To talk health, happiness and prosperity to every person you meet.

To make all your friends feel that there is something in them.

To look at the sunny side of everything and make your optimism come true.

To think only of the best, to work only for the best and expect only the best.

To be just as enthusiastic about the success of others as you are about your own.

To forget the mistakes of the past and press on to greater achievements of the future.

To wear a cheerful countenance at all times and give every living creature you meet a smile.

To give so much time to the improvement of yourself that you have no time to criticize others.

To be too large for worry, too noble for anger, too strong for fear and too happy to permit the presence of trouble.

"Promise Yourself", Christian D. Larson

NEED OR WANT?

Dependency is sometimes the very issue that drives people apart. Partners like to be "counted on" but not a needy "depended on".[44]

Our lives are great when we have someone who enhances our existence, watches out for us, and cares and provides for us. However, if that relationship turns sour and no longer provides what we need, or if in fact it actually takes away from our stroke count, there is a strong likelihood of not only feeling emotionally devastated and empty, but a very real danger of becoming physically ill as well. Our immune system can become compromised when we live too long without a healthy level of strokes. I offer the following encouragement, despite the possibility that most readers will ignore me and keep searching for or expecting that one person to fulfill all their needs:

Do not become dependent on one person, job or activity for the bulk of your stroke needs. Spread your stroke base around to a variety of people and activities.

Even an extremely healthy relationship cannot supply an individual with all their stroke needs. We still need to stroke ourselves for exercising, for being successful at work, having friends, and engaging in a hobby.[45] And we need to continue doing these things, whether or not we are in a relationship.

---

[44] Rosin, *Finding Balance*, p. 101.
[45] Rosin, *Communication & Relationships*, p. 122.

Unhealthy—**NEED**	Healthy—**WANT**
Other person has no choice! All strokes come from this one person.	Other person has a choice!
Even if you get a maximum number of strokes from this person, they cannot supply all your needs and you will still end up in a deficit position. You will have to suck more out of them and risk turning them off. And if they do meet all your needs, they will not be meeting their own—they will not be doing the activities that provide them fulfilment—and will become frustrated. They may then want out of the relationship.[46]	Strokes come from a variety of people and activities.

Quite often, an individual will start a relationship and then stop these activities, and may even stop interacting with other people. They become exclusively dependent on that one person for their strokes, which sets them up for either being controlled by or smothering their partner. Neither work well!

A primary relationship is an important part of life.
Just be careful it does not become your whole life!

---

[46] Rosin, *Finding Balance*, p. 101.

ANTIBODIES AND IMMUNITY

My client insisted on looking through a glass that was half empty, not expecting much from life. He was a good person who did good things for others, but always felt the need to put himself down.

When we use positive self-talk to remain *positive* and *up*, it is like getting a booster shot where antibodies are injected into us to boost our immunity. However, my client was using negative self-talk—his booster shot—to make himself immune to the pain he expected others to inflict on him. He was very hard on himself.

From his perspective, this process was rather successful in that it made him invisible to anything positive he did or was. His plan was to make sure he never became comfortable hearing anything positive. He claimed life was easier this way, and he was clearly not about to change just because he was in my office. Survival with the least amount of pain was his goal. Quality of life was definitely not something he strove for. Just getting through the day was enough success for him.

Is this enough for you, to survive the day? No! Good! Me neither!

**Don't live for the "in case" something bad happens.
Instead, prepare yourself for the best life has to offer.**

STROKES FROM SELF—
WHO WOULD HAVE THOUGHT?!

A client and I were discussing the concept of *strokes* and their importance to one's health. She shared that she had always tried—not all that successfully—to get her strokes from her children, husband and family for "doing" things for them. However, it wasn't working. Her *stroke pot*[47] was empty and she was back to being depressed. She had previously suffered from bouts of depression; this time around, she even spoke of suicide.

We talked further about the physiological need for strokes. From my own perspective, it seemed that she had narrowly defined and structured what she would allow to be counted as a stroke. From her perspective, it was only those strokes received from her teenagers or husband that really counted. She laughed when I resorted to my favourite "let me get this straight (stupid)" routine.

"You mean that you wait until you receive strokes from your hormonally challenged and perpetually miserable teenagers? Or from your managerialdriven husband, who works on average 15 hours of overtime every week? Hmm?" She laughed at the irony of the situation and stated that she was now getting closer to accepting the main idea—that if she were to "get her pot filled" then she would have to fill it herself!

I used the analogy of a turn-of-the-century farmer who was compelled to provide for all of his family's needs. In order to survive and remain healthy for another year, he had to plant all the grain and vegetables, raise all the meat, and harvest and preserve everything that he and his family would need.

---

[47] Virginia Satir, *Peoplemaking*, Paula Alto, CA, Science and Behavior Books, Inc., 1972.

I pointed out that she was in much the same situation as the farmer—if she didn't provide for herself, she, too, would starve. As such, she needed to give herself strokes, so as to stay healthy.

She now understood that if she was going to raise her *stroke count* up to a healthy level, she would need to start counting those strokes that she had been prone to ignore. Strokes for "who she was", "what she did" (including what she did for her own family), and "how well she took care of herself". We agreed that in order to "stroke" herself, these were the new criteria she would use from now on!

This lady needed to overcome two very strong societal dictates before she could provide herself with the strokes she needed. One, she needed to truly understand that giving strokes to herself isn't just okay, it is imperative; and two, she needed to appreciate that it is okay to give yourself strokes for doing fun and relaxing activities. In fact, fun self-care activities ought to have the highest stroke value!

I believe 80% of the strokes we need to be healthy have to come from ourselves![48]

---

[48] Rosin, *Finding Balance,* p. 102.

HUMBLE GONE BAD

I found myself being quite supportive of my client for the reason that some of her behaviours, in particular her self-effacing style, seemed to mirror my own disposition. Maybe *I* needed to see a therapist.

At least in the beginning of our sessions, I found myself reframing many of her shy and humble responses as positive character traits. She had learned to focus on helping others, with little concern for herself. She was a Rescuer[49] with a poor self-image.

On the whole, she was a wonderful, loving, caring and concerned individual toward others. Unfortunately, she was very much less inclined toward herself. She had no concept of the need for self-care. She did not give herself strokes for being the really good person she was or for the good deeds she did. As a result, she had become somewhat resentful. "Everyone seems to get what they want, but nobody asks me what I want!"

She was, in fact, *stroke deprived,*[50] which contributed to her vulnerability and led to her being easily hurt. She certainly couldn't be accused of being conceited or prideful, which was a fear she had brought with her from early child and adolescent experiences. A fear predicated on her belief that "conceited people aren't well thought of". As a result, she would rarely ever acknowledge her own positive qualities and certainly never speak of them. She would easily reward others, but never herself. Was she ready for a change?

I see so many individuals where poor self-esteem is at the root of their issues. In fact, I have come to believe that low self-esteem is the single largest factor behind most personal problems. We are experiencing an absolute epidemic of individuals with this "condition"—I don't know what else to call it: People coming out of their adolescence thinking poorly of themselves and with fairly clear directives from various *systems*— school, community, society, church, and quite often even their parents—to

---

[49] Rosin, *Finding Balance,* p. 63.
[50] Rosin, *Finding Balance,* p. 63.

discount their abilities, accomplishments and their very personhood, in favour of being humble and learning to live with few positive strokes and little self-care. They have what it takes to make it in today's world, but are not given enough encouragement to believe in themselves. What is clear to me is that with so many feeling so poorly about themselves, we will all pay as a society.

Paraphrasing Hans Selye, "The reason you take care of yourself first is so you can then take better care of others." My client needed to hear this kind of permission several hundred times before she would allow herself to even consider what it would mean to her life if she were given permission to take care of herself. Guess what her homework was? Her two new mottos were:

> **"You're first in line for my strokes—right after me!"**
> **"If you've got it, flaunt it!"**
> **(And collect all the strokes you can for it, guilt-free!)**

MUDDIED WATERS

We can't live our lives fully or with gusto without our Fun Child (FC)[51]—that part of us that laughs and seeks out adventure, is creative and mischievous, and thoroughly enjoys most of what life has to offer. There is, however, a side to the (FC) that is very disturbing to the Critical Parent (CP) part that has all the answers to how life *should* and *must be*. And because the (FC) seeks out entertainment and does not concern itself with analysing situations for what is appropriate, the (CP) in other people often gets annoyed at what they see as an *irresponsible person*. I think this judging of the individual is where some of the self-esteem issues referred to in the previous concept—"Humble Gone Bad"—originate from.

In adolescence and early adulthood, the (CP) passes on a great many messages to the inner (FC) that it is not acting in an appropriate manner. In response, the (FC) passes on a great many *unworthy messages* to self that are quite significant and destructive. The Adult (A)—that part of the person that works off logic (with very little emotion) to determine the most appropriate response to the messages being received between the many parts—is most often needed to counteract and challenge the unworthy messages that the Child (C) gives to self and receives from the (CP).

The (A)'s influence in the *present* is greatly influenced by the damaged (C) from the *past*. Poor self-image resides mostly in the (C) and certainly affects the logistical work of the (A).

The (C) muddies the logistical water of the (A).

---

[51] Eric Berne, *Games People Play*, New York, NY, Grove Press, 1964, p. 25.

STINGY WITH STROKES

During a therapy session, I felt it appropriate to share my *Conscientious Objector* (CO) story with a client.[52]

Apparently, during World War II, a number of these COs were interred as prisoners and subjected to experiments involving starvation by their own government. What was significant, and the reason for the story, was that these prisoners had so tuned their body to an absolute minimum of food that they could literally suck nourishment out of nothing and survive.

My client's issue was with her *difficult* teenager who was emotionally very closed and stingy with his positive comments—strokes.[53] Because she personalized his behaviour, she continuously hurt herself.

I shared the CO story with her and then asked her why I had shared it. She replied that it was to convey the principle of obtaining emotional peace and comfort from even the most modest morsel of nourishment that her son passed on to her. Unfortunately, knowing what she could do didn't change things, and she continued to hurt herself because of his behaviour.

We talked about *how to live better with less.* Then we focused on how to brush off her son's negative comments and poor attitude, and recycle any of the positive feedback that he shared—even the smallest morsel. I also suggested that she dramatically increase her output of strokes toward him. Perhaps his responsiveness toward her would change if she responded more positively to him.

It is true that bouquets from teenagers are few and far between, and we'd best hold on to them dearly when they do come our way. We need to glean our positive strokes much like the COs gleaned their nourishment 70 plus years ago.

Many teenagers (and parents) don't mean to be so stingy with their positive strokes and often don't withhold them on purpose. Perhaps they don't feel so good about themselves or have been poorly treated, and

---

[52] Rosin, *Finding Balance,* p. 90.
[53] Rosin, *Finding Balance,* p. 94.

don't have anything extra to share. Some teenagers, however, have an oversized sense of entitlement. And when their guardians disagree with their decisions, they feel they have the right to make their guardians' lives hell. This hell thing goes both ways.

> *On some days, just surviving the day is all we're going to get. The silence we receive and the fact that we are not being criticized can be reframed into a positive stroke. A smile or eye contact is like winning the lottery.*

She was beginning to understand that even the most benign comment from her teenager needed to be accepted and given full value. In terms of value, it could actually be given twice the stroke value! She felt better knowing that both her feelings and those of her teenager were normal.

Take what the day gives you and call it a banquet!

BELIEFS DRIVE BEHAVIOUR

What a person believes about self has an incredible influence on their behaviour. Most behaviours flow from one's belief system. If we want to change behaviour, it follows that we must first identify and then challenge the belief that drives that behaviour.

Example: If I have been influenced to believe that *I am not worthwhile*, then my self-esteem will be low and my behaviour will reflect that belief, and:

a. I analyse myself/others/everything too much, and come up with the proof that supports my negative beliefs.
b. Everything is thought out well in advance, with little flexibility and much rigidity. Spontaneity is nonexistent and I have no trust that I can just do it.
c. Everything is thought out using superfluous hindsight. I go over everything I did and criticize myself as a way to support irrational beliefs that I am not worthwhile.
d. I over-explain, because I feel that people don't understand my poorly worded explanations.
e. I recycle negative comments that prove my sense that I am not worthy.
f. I overreact—I either become paralysed or I attack.

> **Watch your thoughts; they become words.**
> **Watch your words; they become actions.**
> **Watch your actions; they become habits.**
> **Watch your habits; they become character.**
> **Watch your character; it becomes your destiny.**

IRRATIONAL FEELINGS AND BELIEFS

It sometimes helps to know that our thoughts and feelings are irrational *remnants*. These remnants most often come from a previous life as a member of a dysfunctional family.

As my clients have so aptly put it, "These thoughts make it hard to reach out to people. I have been hurt many times and I am not very trusting. I don't make new friends easily and feel that if they really knew me, they wouldn't like me."

In these situations, I make every attempt to have my clients separate their past irrational thoughts and feelings about themselves from their present behaviours—often not so easy to do!

Irrational thoughts, feelings and beliefs are leftovers or holdovers from early experiences where we drew conclusions about ourselves and decided how best to survive our Family of Origin. We all struggle with the results of those early decisions and the inadequate coping strategies that develop.

Beliefs and feelings dictate behaviours.

It therefore becomes very important that we understand that our feelings and beliefs—about ourselves and about others—*leak out* in our behaviour. The most important response to these irrational and antiquated thoughts and behaviours is to short circuit and challenge them. Remember that they limit us from *being all we can be*. In the process of separating the irrational feelings and behaviours—those which must be changed—from those that *make sense* and need to stay in our lives, we end up with behaviours that best meet our needs.

My experience tells me that when you start to work at challenging these old thoughts, feelings and beliefs, it will be important for you to remember that you must change your usual response by doing something totally different. And it is important to differentiate between doing something *different* and doing something *correct*.

Don't wait for the *correct* response in order to start changing. Start the change process by using a different response, and eventually you'll find the one that is the best fit for you!

Keep the following four steps in the back of your mind:

1. *Recognize* (the old response)
2. *Don't accept* (the old response)
3. *Challenge* (the old response)
4. *Create* (a new response)

Listed below are a few great examples of some irrational feelings and beliefs, and how you can challenge them and substitute positive and healthy thoughts and behaviours.

1a. Belief (–)

"Life is hard and then you die!"
You are powerless against the forces of heredity, environment and childhood lessons.

What behaviours result from this belief?

_____
_____
_____
_____

1b. Belief (+)

"Life is what you make it!"
You have the power to change.
You have the power to be whomever you want.

What behaviours result from this belief?

_____
_____
_____
_____

2a. Belief (–)
"I am quite powerless against the wants and needs of others. They come first!"

What behaviours result from this belief?

_____
_____
_____
_____

2b. Belief (+)
"I am 'in charge' and responsible for having a 'good or bad' life!"

What behaviours result from this belief?

_____
_____
_____
_____

3a. Belief (–)
"I am not very smart!"

What behaviours result from this belief?

_____
_____
_____
_____

3b. Belief (+)
"I am intelligent, capable, and can accomplish most anything I set my mind to!"

What behaviours result from this belief?
___
___
___
___

**It really does make a significant difference
in your behaviour if your mindset is positive.
But, of course, you already knew that!**

FILTER

She had been carrying and telling her story for more than 40 years. When I asked if it felt like a life sentence, she readily agreed.

We then both agreed that she would tell her story one last time in writing. She would share with me the highlights/ lowlights, or where she was stuck, and then that would be it! She would no longer need the old story with its "limiting" history to define who she was. She needed to find out who she "is" and to enjoy the present and future.

Our goal was to lose the old *Filter of Expectation* that she had been using to define her life and to create a new *Filter of Permission* to enjoy life.

(Old) Filter of Expectation	(New) Filter of Permission
Based on early life experiences	Based on the current belief that I deserve to enjoy life
Unfortunately, all present experiences are run through these old feelings, words, sayings and scripts.	New Promise Pleasure Permission "to do"
Stoppers, limiters "Be afraid"	"Be curious and fun loving"

Tell your story! Individual therapy! Group therapy! Writing classes! Whatever it takes so that you can get it off your chest and become healthy. Tell yourself that you are sick and tired of telling (and living) the same, sad old story! It is understood that if you share your "story" with at least one other person and they believe you (please pick someone who will believe you), then your story is considered valid and you can let it go!

Give yourself permission to be happy, enjoy life and to love who you are. And then tell this new story again and again!

GOOD GUILT

I am not a promoter of guilt because I consider it quite a destructive emotion. However, if used in the right manner, it can act as a deterrent, help to catch people's attention, and prevent them from doing worse things than feeling guilty. For example, when couples stop feeling guilty for treating each other so poorly, I warn them that "they are getting into very dangerous territory"—that of not caring at all.

They were continually sniping at each other. Everything had become a confrontation because they refused to back down from the other person. Every conversation turned into a clash where they went for the jugular. They remembered every put-down and every negative comment that the other ever uttered during their relationship, and responded back in kind.

Despite the conflict, however, they really did love each other. They seemed to know exactly what they were doing, and in therapy would actually laugh about how ridiculously they were treating each other. Individually, they were delightful people; together, they were *emotional dynamite*.

I advised them to "be careful of your responses to each other. They are becoming progressively meaner and there appears to be fewer boundaries. You no longer feel bad when you *zap* each other. In fact, quite the opposite; you seem to feel vindicated."

I delivered the "I am not a promoter of guilt" speech, and proceeded to point out just how dangerous it was to feel no guilt about their behaviour.

> *To let all your feelings out because you feel like it or, in your estimation, because the other person deserves it, is destructive behaviour that will eventually cost you your relationship.*

They listened and, I am not particularly proud to say, felt a tiny bit guilty about how I used the topic of guilt to get their attention. They said they knew their behaviour was very dangerous and asked for skills to improve their situation. Now you're talking!

If used in the right manner, "guilty talk" can act as a deterrent to help catch people's attention, and even prevent them from doing or saying worse things.

CLEAN SLATE

Every day when we wake up we begin with a clean slate. We clear away the things we don't like. Things we have said or done, our errors, the discounting of self and others. All wiped clean. Good concept, eh? Easy in theory, perhaps, but not easy in practice. As humans, we are more prone to wiping our slates clean when it comes to the good things in life, and holding on to the mistakes or the faux pas we make. In order to wipe the slate completely clean, an "apology" for our actions is often required. Apologizing seems to be the most prevalent way of wiping the slate clean. We operate on the belief that if we apologize, we are somehow forgiven for our bad deeds and entitled to start over with the person to whom we have done wrong. This need to obtain people's forgiveness so we can "feel okay" can become an obsession.

We have this imperfect moment, like when we say, "No, I can't do that for you", and then we feel guilty about it afterward. In modern society, it is apparently not socially acceptable to refuse a request without an elaborate excuse and an apology. Or maybe it's just in Canada. So, the only way we return to feeling comfortable with ourselves and to sleep at night is to apologize and throw our comfort level before the other person's mercy.

This false premise—that we were put on this earth to meet everyone else's needs or there will be a stain on our slate—has resulted in a mistaken belief that "Only when we do for others or sacrifice ourselves will we be acceptable, worthy and okay!" Argh!

Starting each new day fresh, with a clean slate, sounds like a good thing to me. But only if the criterion upon which we do so is based on the understanding that "It's a new day." It doesn't really work if we are trying to clean the slate by making up for all the real and perceived mistakes that we made on the previous day, i.e., further apologies, or with a view to eliminate our guilt based on some dysfunctional need to take care of other people's needs, wants and demands. Let's make each day a new day and not have to "square it right" with the contacts from the previous day.

Stop feeling guilty all the time!
Stop pleasing others all the time!
Let yesterday go while drawing upon the good of this day!
Do the best you can and start each day fresh!

GUILT—A TEACHING TOOL

Guilt is an emotion. Almost everyone *feels guilty* about something sometime in their lives. It is a feeling that is taught through the stories, words and behaviours of both our family and the social groups that we grow up in. These groups believe that how they were taught to understand the world is the correct way, and it is their responsibility to pass on this truth to their children. They believe in a way that they have Universal Truth.[54]

Most often guilt is taught through the use of *feel bad words* by well-meaning people—parents, school, religious groups—whose intention it is to provide children with proper values and have them practise *acceptable* behaviours. They want to give them the formula on how to make it through life using guilt as the teacher.

However, this formula generally insists that group needs be put first and individual needs second. Behind all of the societal directives that come from this formula is the reinforcement to do less for self and more for others. This is why so many *caretakers* do not take care of themselves and eventually burn out. In our modern society, many people buy into the others first value outright and feel a great deal of guilt when they do take care of themselves.

While not my favourite emotion, good guilt can sometimes be used to persuade people to choose a better path, do the proper thing, and make the appropriate decisions.

Young children (mainly under 11) do not have the ability to think rationally and logically, and require guidance from the more mature adults in their lives. Hopefully, these adults have the young person's best interests at heart, but we know that in some families, this isn't always the case. Instead of being used as a teaching tool with mostly positive results, guilt is often used to control the young person.

---

[54] Rosin, *Finding Balance,* p. 84.

Guilt can be a positive teaching tool or a method of control, depending on the intent of the "teacher." Most of the guilt lessons that are taught to us by our parents, at school, and in religious settings are intended to serve as guides for acceptable behaviours.

Once we have the ability to think rationally and logically for ourselves (generally after ages 11 to 13), we can then decide which of the directives (that we have been hearing all our lives) are best for us, and feel less guilty about whatever choice we make. We can be aware and careful to avoid introducing these same negative cycles of guilt into our own parenting style when we have children of our own.

"Good Guilt" can be reframed to teach, remind, and emphasize the "important things" in life, like health and happiness.

ANGER AND ASSUMPTIONS

A client relayed a recent experience in which he was cooperating on an important work project with an individual whom he felt was a "bit of a slacker". Whenever this individual heard the phone ringing in the adjoining office, he immediately jumped up to answer it. My client assumed that the individual was using the ringing telephone as an excuse to get out of work, and he became very angry, uttering a few expletives under his breath.

When returning from one of his telephone excursions, this individual apologized and said that he had been expecting a call about his very ill father. My client felt embarrassed and very relieved that the person had not heard his inappropriate expressions of anger—a response that was based entirely on a false assumption.

Making an assumption about what someone says or does, without understanding their motivation or having all the facts, can lead to knee-jerk responses, frustration, agitation, anger and hurt feelings. Assumptions are dangerous, and because they are narrow in scope and made without all the information needed, they are often influenced by how the person making the assumption feels at that moment or by personal beliefs and values.

Quite often, when a person assumes less than positive things about others—causes, decisions, lifestyles, behaviours, beliefs—it is a reflection of that person's own low self-esteem. Those who make the negative assumption generally aren't all that comfortable in their own skin. They see things that aren't there and hear things that aren't true. And these things can be totally off the mark. Making assumptions instead of verifying the truth or checking the facts is a guaranteed way to raise tension in most relationships.

Below is an example from my previous life as a first-year teacher when I thought I knew everything and actually knew very little:

Jim was a good kid, an average student, but one morning he fell asleep in class, my class, my extremely life-altering grade nine geography class. I yelled and embarrassed him. To think he could fall asleep in such an interesting class. Where was his head at? I discovered later that day his grandmother had died the previous night and he hadn't slept at all, but he didn't want to miss school. And I had yelled at him! Where was my head at? That experience influenced me to make fewer assumptions and to check things before opening my mouth—and putting my foot in it. Jim did hear an apology from one very humble teacher, and he did forgive me.

Responding with anger to any situation is a choice. Although there are times when it is appropriate to be angry, in most cases it is best to "talk" about what is causing an angry reaction and not to "be" angry.[55] And it is almost never appropriate to choose anger based on an assumption. Be sure to check things out thoroughly before speaking.

Don't assume anything—get the facts first—then act!

RIGHTEOUS ANGER AND THE QL METER

She had been sick for almost a year. In response to the break-up of her marriage, she had made herself ill with feelings of hopelessness and despair. She kept asking all of the logical *why questions* about his *feelings* and *behaviours*.

I challenged her by continually referring to the fact that, by asking the why questions, she was choosing to maintain her focus on the problem instead of moving on and finding a solution to her life in the present.

She was angry that her relationship woes had cost her a 20 year career in the run up to the divorce. Because she had become too upset and too emotionally distracted to work, they let her go. She was angry at having lost the life she had known and at having to start over. She was angry with her ex-husband for only occasionally being available to their son. She was one very angry lady who had taken to lashing out at everyone—including me!

I bit my tongue for the longest while, but finally, her attitude—one that basically said, "I can dump on everyone because I was treated unfairly by my partner"—was more than I could take. I firmly stated:

> *Stop it! Just because you were dumped doesn't give you the right to abuse all the other people in your life. They didn't dump you; they only want to support you! Besides, staying angry isn't healthy for you. You need to let go of your anger and get on with your life.*

Over the past year, she had refused to hear similar advice from her friends and family, and she certainly didn't wish to hear it from me. She wasn't buying my *logic* and despite several sessions together, she fought the "letting go" and remained stuck in the quagmire of her anger.

As humans, there is something about righteous anger and the desire to hold on to that anger until justice and fairness are restored to us. By now, most of us know that *the world isn't fair*, and yet we continue to act as though it should be, and end up harbouring a great deal of bitterness when we decide that something or someone hasn't been fair. We feel we have a right to maintain that angry position because a wrong was committed against us. We often do not realize or stop to reflect on the fact that by maintaining our focus on our *right* to be angry, we end up harming ourselves.

In the course of my career, I have seen three ways in which people deal with righteous anger. One, they refuse to move on until some form of justice has been enforced—but even though there is justice, quite often it is not enough to restore their sense of well-being.

Two, by holding onto their anger, they see that those who are close to them are suffering and so they decide to give up their search for justice. They go back to concentrating on getting supper, painting the porch, getting the kids to soccer practice, and recapturing the life they may have lost.

And the third category is those individuals who aren't focused on justice at all. They are simply stuck in their anger. They remain stuck because they have no perspective except for *what was*, or *what happened*. They do not seem to be able to create a new way of seeing things. I have heard them say, "I don't know what my life would look like if I gave up my anger. I won't let go of my anger until I have a new vision, and yet I do not seem to be able to create a new vision until I let go of my anger, and so …." Yep, these people really are stuck. The saddest part is that they simply won't allow themselves to be helped.

I would like to invent a *Quality of Life (QL) Meter*. It would measure a person's quality of life in the present and help them negate any past failures, disappointments and angers—especially righteous ones! It wouldn't take people too long to realize that it really didn't make much sense at all to hold onto thoughts, feelings, values and beliefs that didn't nourish their minds or hearts. And perhaps seeing the results of the meter would remind them what was really important in life. Or perhaps just coming to realize that letting go of the angers and disappointments of life could be the catalyst needed to allow the healing to begin.

In regards to the original, precipitating event that invited the "unfair" label and anger, it no longer matters whose fault it is/was; if you *stay angry*, then you *stay stuck*.

However, if you release *your anger*—talk it out or just decide to let it go—then you can take *back your life* and be free to involve yourself with all aspects of your life.

"Let go—Let Live."
(Sound familiar?)

MORE THAN DISCIPLINE

The couple in my office were angry and very dissatisfied with their relationship. Our first session ended with a discussion on self-discipline as a way of controlling anger.

The next session began with a very positive report: "The discussion we had on discipline is working and we are being much nicer to each other as a result." My immediate thought was jaded: "Yeah, but for how long?" Both spouses brought a great deal of "historic" anger with them— abuse, parental alcoholism— and, to his credit, he admitted, "I am spoiled and used to having my own way!"

They explained that since our previous session, things had been good between them and they had consciously kept their anger—frustration, resentment, paranoia—under control. However, as I investigated further, I found that their interpretation of *self-discipline* meant saying nothing to one another for fear of "rocking" the boat. This certainly was not the long-term answer for their anger problem or for a successful relationship!

Having strong feelings with *no voice* is dysfunctional and potentially explosive. You certainly need self-discipline to control your feelings if a relationship is to be successful. But you also need to have the skills and the desire to "talk things out" with one another. You need to share your feelings and not necessarily "be" them. *Talk about your anger and not be angry!* You need to express your thoughts, feelings, values and beliefs. After all, that is who you are, and you need "to have a voice" in order to be heard and to be healthy.

They reverted back to arguments and fights, and their relationship really got off track. They didn't make a conscious effort to practise healthy self-discipline,[55] they didn't use "I" language,[56] and they didn't listen. They just found fault with each other. The state of their relationship had become even worse than when they had come in for our first session. That

---

[55] Rosin, *Finding Balance*, p. 89.
[56] Rosin, *Finding Balance*, p. 53.

is sometimes the case when people build up expectations for therapy, only to have it be less than they expected. They get very angry, very quickly.

We began again. It was not completely starting over because some healthy lessons had been learned. But we were all a little wiser and the lessons about discipline and "I" language were no longer just theory. As a couple, they realized they had to stay more focused and practise harder the skills of communicating. This time they actually did their homework.

Self-discipline is not enough!
"Willing" your behaviour long term will not work.
A healthy person needs to talk about their feelings,
not "be"—act on—those feelings!

There is a difference between self-discipline and self-denial.
One exercises healthy caution when moving forward; the
other exercises total restraint while standing still.

ANGER

I can't remember the last time a female had been referred to me for anger management issues. Until recently, males seem to have had a monopoly on this issue.

My initial interview with this particular person started out along the lines of, "Tell me why you're here? Why did they refer you to me? What has frightened you or them to bring you here?"

In response, what I heard was how she was often impatient with other people's tendencies to be slow. She was annoyed that people didn't understand or do what she felt was an eminently clear and logical response to a particular situation or set of circumstances. She became very frustrated and angry at people's behaviour and their "obvious" stupidity. Her one consistent response in dealing with people was her anger.

I shared with her my *Golden Rule of Anger*:

You cannot "be" angry. You can only "talk" about your anger.

Her facial expression said, "You're too soon with the Golden Rule crap" and I think she thought I was an idiot.

Her look reminded me of a previous experience. A male was referred to me by the courts for repeatedly abusing his wife. I asked him if he spoke and behaved at work like he did at home. Looking at me as though I were not within my right mind to have even posed such a question, he shot back, "Of course not, I would be fired."

He apparently had the discipline to behave appropriately at work, but not at home. He truly believed his angry outbursts were all her fault: "If she were only (different … quicker … less … more …), then I wouldn't have to get angry."

Anger is a behaviour to be used very sparingly in any relationship because it is harmful and "just doesn't work"

> *in most cases. Hurt, frustration and disappointment are generally what we are feeling, but we short circuit them and go straight to anger. Apparently expressing how you feel—hurt, frustration, disappointment—using "I" statements is much more readily accepted by the listener than being yelled at. Go figure, eh!*

While in certain limited instances, anger can be used as a legitimate and sometimes even positive emotion, I am appalled at how self-centred and self-serving it can be. Intimidation, belligerence, force and brutality against another human being just to get what you want are truly disgusting behaviours! It is too easy to say "I didn't mean it" or "I am sorry" after verbally or physically abusing a loved one, or after intimidating a mild mannered and gentle co-worker.

Generally, the perpetrators don't act that way when the boss is there or the heavy weight is on the shipping floor. Clearly we do have discipline—when we choose to use it!

Indeed, all of life's decisions are about choices, such as how we respond to others—whether with anger or with reason. When I think about all the damage this emotion has done to people's lives just because someone else feels they have the right or know that they can get away with bullying behaviours, I get angry! Perhaps I need to talk with someone!

> *Sometimes I'm not fond of how I respond to certain individuals, like with anger or sarcasm. So I go back to them after a brief rehearsal in my head and start over. After all, there is one person above all whom I want to be proud of me … and that's me!*

Anger is a choice!
 Nobody can make me angry.
  People can invite me to be upset, but I choose whether or not to be angry.
   Can I be invited to feel angry? Yes!
   Made to feel angry? No!

EXPECTATIONS OR ASSERTIVENESS

One needs to set one's own course,
Not follow or be directed by someone else's course,
Because, of course, that will throw you off course.

(Anonymous—because I really
don't want to take credit for it!)

On several occasions, he had expressed anger and confusion because of how people treated him. He had tried so hard to please and satisfy them. He was such a good and loyal friend, but felt that most of the people in his life looked right through him, as though he wasn't even there. He couldn't understand why this was, and I couldn't find the right words to take away his hurt and disappointment.

I knew that it was not going to be easy to convince him that the people in his life didn't wake up each day thinking about how they could make him feel insignificant. It was his behaviours that led to the kinds of reactions he was getting.

The most sensitive advice that I could provide was that most of the problem he was describing was of his own making, but the right words just wouldn't come to assist me in this task. "You're not dynamic enough." "You're too nice." "You're too agreeable." All of them crossed my mind, but I couldn't say anything that would help him understand why he was being taken for granted. Nothing I could think of could help him understand why he had become invisible.

He was one of those really nice, middle-aged men who would do anything for anyone. But it seemed that nobody reciprocated. In social situations, he felt as though he was constantly being ignored and devalued. He wouldn't say anything to those who he felt had wronged him. Instead, he went home to rage in private— to the point of making himself physically sick.

I finally found some words that I thought might help:

You have no ability to say "NO!"
You have no teeth.
There are no consequences if someone offends you.
You say nothing.
You have no voice.

That certainly didn't help!

For homework, I asked him to look at who he was, to examine his positive qualities, and to list them all on a sheet of paper. At the next session, he returned with several pages! After reading them closely, I agreed that he indeed had all of the qualities listed. "You're really a good person, but it seems you don't have a voice!" He agreed.

It was when he held up the page with all his good qualities and behaviours and expressed curtly that most people in his life did not reciprocate with similar behaviours toward him that I realized his anger was grounded in his *"expectations"* for others.

He treated others a certain way—logical and appropriate in his mind—and expected the same toward him. When they didn't, he raged! It was this client's *unrealistic expectations* for people, combined with a *lack of assertiveness* in dealing with others, that led to his *rage*.

EXPECTATIONS	ASSERTIVENESS
I put others "in charge" of my needs	**I am "in charge" of my needs**

We agreed:

- *If you want to be heard, you need "a voice".*
- *If you use your voice and they still don't listen, you need to be firmly assertive.*
- *If you're firmly assertive and they still don't listen, then the consequences will most likely be a failed relationship.*

He stated that having expectations for others and needing them to act a certain way for him to be "okay"— without a voice—had left him feeling frustrated and vulnerable. Without the ability to appropriately challenge others and defend himself, there were little to no consequences for others' actions toward him. As a result, they thoughtlessly dismissed and ignored him.

His response to our discussion was, "I absolutely need to have the ability to challenge and be heard by the people in my life, or they won't even know—or care—that I am alive!"

Being nice without a voice doesn't cut it!

FINDING YOUR VOICE

She was very timid. For the longest time, she wouldn't look me in the eye and her voice lacked emotion. Most of her conversation was made up of questions instead of statements, and even then, for every question she asked, she immediately apologized.

Later, I heard about the past abuse in her life. She said that she was "fed up being a doormat". She wanted to change and get more out of life. She had learned early on that the only way to survive in her family was to be passive. Any other way was seen as a "smart mouth" and punishable.

She grew up without a voice, taking her lead from others. Being passive didn't get her what she wanted, but she didn't want a backhand either. She came to understand that *having a voice,* that speaking your mind, speaking up, being proactive in your life, all had a dark side. Now that she had entered her middle years, she realized that she wanted more from life and that she:

Could not be proactive unless she had a voice!

"If I speak up, it will only make things worse." In the context of her original family, she was probably correct and so didn't learn to speak up. She became timid and shy and withdrew from social contact. She learned to be passive early in her life and was now paying the price. She didn't have a voice, and at the same time was battling the belief that if she found a voice it could make her life worse.

Compounding her fears was her understanding of what having a voice meant. To her, it meant being aggressive with a "take no prisoners" mentality. She was relieved to hear that having a voice could mean being assertive, and that assertiveness meant respecting and listening to the other person's point of view. And that meant having them listen to and respect your perspective as well. She smiled when I put it this way:

A voice is just a voice, not a fist!

I warned her that not everyone in her life would appreciate her quest to find her voice.

> *Sometimes even the people who love you the most will not be thrilled when you say "no" or express an opinion that is different from theirs. And it is important to consider that if this is the way that those who love you react, then imagine how the people who don't love you will react? People often want us to remain predictably the same. Unfortunately for you, that means remaining without a voice. You must realize that this way they will have more control over their lives and over yours as well.*

If one is to become assertive and proactive in the world, One needs to find their voice.

MOTHERS HAVE RIGHTS!

The question "Are problem kids really the result of problem parents?" is the cause of a lot of blame in our society. The blame for the poor behaviour of our youth is principally being placed squarely on the shoulders of parents, and in some cases, rightfully so.

However, there is an unhealthy backlash that is occurring in response to this blame, whereby the *effective* parents who really do care about their kids are sometimes being painted with the same brush as the *ineffective* parents. As a result, many of these effective parents are over-reacting—to avoid being seen as doing too little for their children, they inadvertently do too much for them.

My client was one of those mothers who felt very guilty if she was not constantly doing something for her family—baking cookies, driving kids to their many activities, painting her teenage daughter's room. Consequently, she did not know the meaning of *no* and was close to burning out. She mistakenly thought that sacrificing her own needs and life was the correct way to demonstrate her love for her family. She saw this as proper parenting.

She couldn't understand why she was depressed or why she felt a growing resentment toward her family. And she really couldn't understand the poor behaviour of her children and husband, in spite of the fact that she was doing everything for them. Hmm!

She registered a *nine* on the Richter scale when I informed her that I thought *she* was the problem. With the common guilt that many effective parents use to interpret such feedback, she immediately heard me saying, "You must be doing something bad." But what I was really saying was, "You're doing too much. Haven't you heard that mothers have rights, too?" Then I shared a saying from my youth that referenced her family's behaviour toward her:

"I am not your servant, I am your mother."

I joked with her and made up a story about some mothers in Australia who had banded together and formed a union in which they were entitled to breaks—six weeks of holidays without their kids, all guilt free. She really enjoyed my union story, nervously laughing at points, while letting the possibility seep into her consciousness.

It was sad for me to watch this lady who had never before entertained the thought that she had the right to a life separate from her role as wife and mother. She was frustrated and angry at having to continue in this role, but the guilt—her own inner guilt as well as that dumped on her by her husband and family— helped to maintain the status quo in her household.

At the close of the session, she left my office resolved to become the *union's official representative* in her own home!

We had several good sessions laughing about the surprised responses of her family as she struggled to find her way out of the guilt and rigidity of a belief system where she didn't exist.

Together, we decided, "In any era—either now or a hundred years ago—it isn't easy to be a mother, with rights and 'a life'. But if a woman doesn't believe that she is entitled to such rights, then those around her—even those who love her—won't be too anxious to inform her of those rights!"

Being entitled to your rights doesn't mean family and friends necessarily support your right to "your rights".

Life is simpler and easier for them if you remain a servant and not "a mother with rights".

WHY QUESTIONS?

For many years now, I have stopped asking my clients *why* questions. For the most part, these questions focus on the underlying reason for or the origin of the way that something is or has been.

Now, I ask them *what* they need to change to make their life better in the here and now. If the client's story about the past needs to be told, I will listen! But if the purpose of the story is so the client can better understand why they act the way they do, they will likely hear me say:

> *I am sure that if we examined your background carefully, we would conclude that your present behaviour is understandable and that you have chosen how to conduct your life as best you could under the circumstances. It worked—you're here, and you're a wonderful and fully functioning human being. But something needs to change in the "now". I am wondering if what needs to change/be different has something to do with behaviours you brought with you from your early years, which are no longer working for you? Put simply, your behaviour is understandable, but no longer appropriate.*

My clients and I agree to work on *what* needs to be changed rather than on *why* things are the way they are. It sounds simple, but it isn't! We can so easily become lost in the rigidity of our early *learning* or in our comfort in looking for the *why* we are the way we are. "Why" questions often get asked so that the person doesn't have to change anything— they only look for and are satisfied to know the why of their behaviour.

So, "why" you act the way you do is out; "what" behaviours need changing or will begin to make your life better is in.

I understand that there is a belief that I can only figure out "what" to do when I understand "why" I am the way I am or act the way I do. For me, this understanding of "why" is overrated; while sometimes necessary, mostly it slows down the process of changing.

If you keep doing what you're doing, You'll keep getting what your getting. Focus on "what" needs to be changed and not "why" you have the issue

WHY + WORRY = NO ACTION

People ask "why" questions so they don't have to take action! My client was stuck. She had several sessions where she expressed feelings about her bad relationship with an "uncaring and boorish husband". I asked her what she wanted to do about the situation, and her response, with many variations on the same theme, was, *I'd like 'him' to be different*!

She asked a lot of *why* questions and told a lot of stories, all the while avoiding any *plan of action*.

I surmised that she didn't actually want to change anything; she just wanted to complain about everything!

In all honesty, however, she did want things to change. But she wanted *him* to change, and was afraid that if she actually pushed for change or challenged his behaviour, it would only *make things worse*. So, she chose to complain, hoping that I would precipitate the change in him. "Uh, oh!" and "Oh, no!"

The same kernel of logic that applies to *why* questions can be applied to the act of *worrying*. People often choose to worry about things instead of confronting them and developing a plan of action. The end result is frequently the same for those people who chose to ask *why* questions and *worry* about the answers—they end up taking no action whatsoever.

Don't make a Plan of Action... Just ask a lot of meaningless questions... Worry incessantly until the action feeling passes...
– Not!

I DON'T NEED YOU TO BE DIFFERENT FOR ME TO BE OKAY!

If he would only be less bossy, I would enjoy my day more. If she would only quit gossiping and do her job, then I could do mine better!

There are millions of examples of how our lives would be better, *if only* others would be *different*. Well, I have some bad news! They are not about to change in order to make your life better.

The good news, however, is that you don't have to wait until you know why they act the way they do, or until they actually change their behaviour, before you can feel better. You can just *decide* to feel better about your life!

She was being yelled at on a regular basis by a male co-worker who had been terrorizing people in the office for years. She wondered how much longer she could find the energy to continue working under these circumstances. She pondered how she could change the individual—not possible—and make the workplace a more positive place to work. Fat chance!

Like her co-workers, her style when confronted with this man's irrational behaviour was a need to find out "Why?"

"Why does he act this way? Why does he yell at people? Why hasn't anybody tried to stop him? Why do I take it?"[57]

I asked her to consider dropping all of the "whys" about her co-worker, and instead just invite him to stop. If someone is beating on my head, I really don't care why they are doing it; just stop doing it!

When dealing with irrational people, asking "why" is like pouring gasoline on a fire! This is because when you ask the "why" question, you give them an opening to tell you "why" from their irrational perspective.

---

[57] Rosin, *Communication & Relationships*, p. 157.

This often allows them to justify the very behaviour that you want them to stop.

Begrudgingly she agreed to stop asking the "why" questions. Her agreement with my counsel resided mainly at the intellectual level. She could clearly see the benefits to stopping the parade of questions. "It makes sense!" Emotionally, however, she still resisted. She felt that she needed to know the "intellectual why" before a "behavioural change" was possible. That isn't my experience.

After much discussion on change and, after arriving at the conclusion that we can only change ourselves, my client made a decision to give up her efforts to try to change her co-worker. We then invented a system that would allow her to confront his bullying behaviour with empathy. From that point on, she was to visualize her co-worker as a "sick puppy"—cute, fuzzy and adorable, but sick. After all, who gets angry at a sick puppy? She decided to be satisfied with expressing her thoughts, feelings, values and beliefs on how she felt about being treated poorly. She understood that she could not control if he or others in her life changed, but letting them know how their behaviour was affecting her was entirely within her power. She did it! Wow!

A person's power resides in their own ability to state what they think, feel, value and believe— not in getting others to change!

STRESS AND SEROTONIN

The human body is a remarkable vessel that is complex beyond comprehension. When one of its *systems* becomes impaired due to injury or illness, our body has the ability to "pick up the slack" by using one of its other systems to compensate. A good example of this is when we lose our vision. Automatically, our hearing and intuition improves. However, one of the few systems that does not have an alternative backup mechanism is when we are compelled to deal with stress. When under stress, either real or perceived, the body not only doesn't produce more of the hormones—Serotonin and Dopamine—that are required to deal with this higher level of stress, but it actually cuts back their production and sometimes stops producing them altogether.

My background in biological science is weak, so I won't pretend to understand nor try to explain the cellular workings of the natural *upper* hormones that are found in the brain. I do know, however, that Serotonin and Dopamine are responsible for our being upbeat.

When we are *under stress*, the body stops producing these hormones and we feel flat. As mentioned, the system doesn't adjust and our body doesn't make up for these absent hormones. In fact, we experience a double whammy!

First, the stressful situation itself weighs heavily upon us, and second, we are then forced to carry on without these vital hormones. If the stressful situation is perceived to continue for an extended period of time, we could become depressed.

There is no simple solution to stress. Still, that hasn't stopped hundreds of authors from selling their books to explain what you can do to reduce the stress in your life. And although I just said there is no simple solution, here I am about to give you one.

The simplest methods that anyone can use to compensate for the depletion of Serotonin and Dopamine are:

You can change the stress level in your life by getting rid of some of the negatives—change your address, quit your job, fire your backstabbing friend.

Or

You can change your perception of what is stressful by taking better care of yourself—eat better, exercise more, create more networks of friends, find more to laugh about.

Or

Both!

Or

Take pills—antidepressants.

Laughter is a reflex;
it's a free pharmacy of serotonin and dopamine.

WHICH HOOK?

I rarely ask "why" questions, but here is one I get asked, "Why is it so hard for people to take care of themselves?"

My answer was simple. There are too many *work hard* messages programmed into our on-board computer—the mind. These messages mainly originate from the environment in which we were raised—Family of Origin—beginning with household chores, endless encouragements to get a part-time job throughout high school while maintaining an exceedingly high grade point average, having our future career path planned out by the time we receive our diplomas, and many more directives on how to make it in life. There is often not enough *permission* to go out, play and enjoy life.

The way North American society has been evolving, with all of its existing mentalities—that everyone must work hard; be motivated, driven and ambitious; accomplish more with less; and measure our status based on a bigger house and bigger car—it's no wonder that stress has become a *white noise* word in the lexicon of modern society. The scariness of stress as a negative influence or factor has largely lost its meaning in a day and age that normalizes stress management courses as merely the cost of doing business, nothing special.

More and more, the symptoms of stress have lost the ability to warn people to make better choices in their lives. People have stopped seeing their stressful lifestyles as something they need to work on and get under control. They have accepted the stress in their lives as a *given*. And it is often a given, until they get sick. "What can I do to feel better," they ask? I respond by asking them, "Which of these imaginary hooks would you like to hang your life on?"—and then we get started!

J	J
Accomplishment, Driven, Pursuit of "Things"	Health/Wellness/Balance Quality of Life

I have found that most stressed out/burned out people start out in therapy very well, then, unfortunately, as they get better, revert back to old, not so healthy behaviours. No! We do all the right things—eat properly, exercise, establish good sleep patterns, laugh with friends—until we feel better, and then revert to our old stressful ways. The stress management/wellness lifestyle behaviours are a long-term commitment to staying healthy.[59]

Remember that on the road of life, most objects in the mirror appear smaller than they are! This can be a costly mistake.

IT'S JUST A TV SHOW

I had been listening to the television for only a short time when the young female actress on the screen said to a police officer, "I think I was the first person who ever loved him and I just wanted to show him he mattered."

I shook my head somewhat judgementally. It was a run-of-the mill police drama and on this particular episode, her boyfriend had killed only one person—conservative by today's television violence standards. But the results of the police interview sounded very familiar to me, and I began to heat up.

The girlfriend was feeling guilty for not loving her "poor excuse for a human being" boyfriend enough. I had heard this guilty script from my female clients many times over the years. As with this fictional TV character, they often believed that if they had only cared more, they could have saved or changed their partner.

In my disgust, I shouted at the TV personality, "Oh, stop taking responsibility for his behaviour, and for heaven's sake get a life!" Only an unhealthy person would stay with or make excuses for such an unhealthy partner.

I continued to rant. "Stop looking for such above average dysfunctional men to rescue, just so you can feel needed." I was on a sarcastic roll and there was no stopping me! "Learn to get the strokes you need from having 'a life' and not from rescuing[60] flawed men."

As soon as I realized I was shouting at the television, I stopped, somewhat embarrassed. Like a hurricane, I felt like I had blown myself out. And yet, I wondered why I was getting so excited about a TV show. Was I angry with the women who want to rescue and take responsibility for the inadequate and irresponsible men in their lives? Or was I angry at men because I realize just how often we weasel out of taking responsibility for our actions, inviting the women in our lives to feel guilty about that? As I said before— never mind why, just stop being angry. It's only a TV show, right?

**The first rule for saving someone who is drowning
is to make sure they do not drag you down with them!**

DON'T TRUST, DON'T SHARE, AND DON'T GET CLOSE!

The couple was very tentative as they entered my office. They identified the major problem in their relationship as communication. When they sat down, they were almost turned in opposite directions. Although it seemed that they had already given up on each other, here they were, asking for help.

We talked about how each saw the other and what they thought the problem was. They shared the hurt they felt at the other's words and actions and indicated they had both shut down—emotionally and in their communication—because it was less painful for them.

The session seemed to be moving along very well and I was able to get a good sense of their relationship. They appeared to be building trust between themselves and with me—so important to the counselling process.

Three-quarters of the way through the session, she became very quiet, turned to me and shared her secret: "I can't allow myself to get too close to him because then I will start to really care about him again. I am vulnerable. If I give him power over me, he will take advantage of the situation or I will interpret his behaviour as being hurtful to me in some way. I don't trust him and couldn't handle his rejection again. Therefore, I won't allow myself to get close to him, or allow him to get too close to me."

He was stunned by her insight and ability to articulate her fears. After a moment, he said, "Me, too!" I asked her if she had been so acutely aware of her secret before starting the session, and she replied, "No, it just occurred to me now!" Wow!

There was still a lot of work to be done, but with that level of honesty and sophistication, a positive tone had been set and I was very hopeful for that couple.

Openness and honesty lead to improved trust, improved communication, and a more successful relationship.

HOW MANY CHANCES SHOULD I GIVE YOU?

So much has been written about sex and power. About how sex, or the demand for it, is not really about pleasure derived from the act, but more about power over another person. Personally, I like pleasure part!

I recall a couple that sought my assistance on this issue. He was very arrogant. A demanding individual whose personal motto could have been "My way or the highway!" He believed that "No woman is going to tell me how to live my life. When I want sex, I want it, and I expect you to provide it—or else I'll get mad and freeze you out!"

She, by contrast, although having a healthy libido, felt she didn't have a choice in the relationship when it came to sex. She felt highly disrespected and unloved, and basically responded with "Damn it! This is my body and you can't force me (any longer) with your anger and coldness to do what I don't want to do!" Sound familiar? The controlling behaviours of anger and coldness are a particularly common position taken by one partner or the other. The war was on and both parties felt justified!

Surprisingly, I discovered that the guy had a decent side to him. At times, he understood, was honest and considerate. But there was also a dangerously "child-like" side that operated solely on feelings—needing power and dominance to make up for a poor self-image.

He and I spent a fair amount of time constructing two different positions—*Control Man* and *Mature Man*. I encouraged him to ask himself these questions:

- "*Who's in charge at this moment, Control Man or Mature Man?*"
- "*Who do you want in charge, Control Man or Mature Man?*"
- "*How would Control Man handle this issue? Mature Man?*"

He did some good work and there were distinct changes in his behaviour. But, as often happens with males when they get high, he ended up abandoning all of the progress we had made, said "Screw it!", made some unrealistic demands, and she decided "enough was enough" and left.

It was not over! Some humans trap themselves in a never ending game of "beginnings and endings".

> *"I am sorry. I promise I will never do that to you again."*
> *"Well, okay, as long as you promise to never do that again!"*

I got to thinking about people who stay in relationships where they get abused and discounted. "Because I love him/her," they say. But I say it's because they don't love themselves nearly enough! Because they have low self-esteem, because they think nobody else will ever love them, because if they only "tried harder" he/she would then love them and treat them better. I don't think so!

I am often asked, "Should I give partners, family members, work colleagues, or anyone for that matter, who treats me poorly more chances? How many chances? Any chances?" It wouldn't matter what I said because there are always extenuating circumstances that need to be taken into consideration. There can't be an absolute rule for this issue.

However, I will say—and it's only common sense—that humans make mistakes, occasionally, and we need to forgive and renew our vows of love and "move on". If the behaviour becomes "several", and then "many", the recipient needs to communicate in a "proper manner"[58] that this is unacceptable and there will be consequences[59] if it continues.

All too often people hurl consequences at each other in anger, hoping this behaviour will motivate the other person to agree with their perspective; it doesn't, and nothing changes. It's okay to talk about feelings of anger, but one can't "be" angry because *anger only begets more anger and defensiveness*. Let's give our partners and the significant people in our lives lots of chances, lots of forgiveness, lots of love, and lots of opportunity to learn new skills—topical groups, counselling, reading materials.

There is an old saying, "If you keep doing what you're doing, you'll keep getting what you're getting." If there is no effort to change, to grow, or to understand that there are two people who need to get their needs met in the relationship—and it is a delicate balance—then chances are it will end badly or be eternally unsatisfying.

Every issue and problem comes back to self-esteem!

---

[58] Rosin, *Finding Balance*, p. 63.
[59] Rosin, *Communication & Relationships*, p. 16.

NEW BIG THREE

I call *Ego, Perfection* and *Control* the old dysfunctional *Big Three*. I say old because these are the primary issues I have been seeing in my clients for several decades.

They are the common behaviours of *driven* people who have forgotten how to have fun and often end up making themselves sick in the process. They are not able to acknowledge that although work is good, having a *balanced life* is better!

I know that I have a tendency to react strongly to the what I consider to be unrealistic expectations of the workplace on my clients, but I react even more forcefully to the poor choices that people often make when it comes to taking care of themselves.

In order to counteract the old dysfunctional Big Three, I propose that my clients adopt a new *Big Three* to improve their lifestyles—more *Networking* (with fun people), more *Exercise* (nutrition and sleep), and more *Laughter*!

**Let's build a life based more on fun and enjoyment.
Let's invite more people into our life
who are consistent with our new "Big Three",
and let's fire those who aren't.**

TREATING "PANIC ATTACKS"

I continue to work therapeutically with Panic Attacks as if they are allies.

> *"It is believed in some circles that panic attacks are really allies, and in some bizarre way, attempting to protect and help us. The intent is positive, but the methodology is painful, and the 'help' is dubious."*[60]

It is not an easy sell to convince people that their panic attacks are only trying to keep them safe. So I reframe the attack as a reminder to the person that they need to continue to take good care of themself and remain diligent in maintaining a healthy lifestyle. Two simple techniques I encourage them to practise when confronted by a panic attack are *Self-Talk* and *Anchoring*.

Self-Talk is talking positively to yourself. It is a good strategy to start self-talk as soon as you feel anxious. "Thank-you, panic attack, for reminding me to take steps to take better care of myself and to continue to be diligent in how I design my own positive lifestyle." Use words that acknowledge that the anxiety is an ally and is merely giving you a positive reminder.

Anchoring is touching a spot on the hand or face and thinking—anchoring—a positive thought to that spot. I generally place the thumb of one hand on the Snuff Box (the little hollow between your thumb and index finger) of the other hand. I suggest that people focus in their minds on positive feelings about a place or event where they have felt completely safe, comfortable and loved. I ask them to repeat this technique several times a day, until the mere touching of the anchor spot floods the person with those safe and pleasant feelings. The anchor spot can then be used

---

[60] Rosin, *Finding Balance*, p. 58.

prior to an attack or the next time the person experiences panic. It becomes a "natural pill".

These two techniques are quite safe and effective. However, you won't find any quick fixes for panic attacks from a book, not even this one. Please seek medical/psychological help with your panic attack issues.

Enemy or Ally—you decide!

PREACHING

Preaching is preaching, whether it's done from the pulpit or from the therapist's chair.

It is not my intention to go into details about the right or the wrong, the helpful or the hurtful aspects of preaching and counselling. I'll just own up to the fact that I have spent many years in the counsellor's chair and that I have done it occasionally—preached at my clients! Not often mind you, only when needed—ah, so arrogantly put!

I have disguised many a *sermon* under the guise of "I am only discussing options and alternatives with you", which is standard counsellor "speak". I am even sure that what has sometimes leaked out of my mouth is my own personal philosophy and life position. This has been both helpful and useless, depending upon the situation and the person.

I recall one client who predominantly sought direction and answers for his life not from me but the Bible (good choice). I did my very best to keep my own beliefs out of the session, and instead focused on listening and understanding his world. After several sessions with him and no contract as to where he wanted to go, it became evident that no matter what the issue, his answer to all his problems was God.

During one session, he corrected me at least 26 times for having incorrectly interpreted what he had said. I tried to explore options, but his consistent response was, "God will take care of me." He insinuated that I knew very little about what would help him and that I was a poor listener. In between the 26th and 27th correction, my patience and professional decorum snapped—just a little snap—and out popped my *"Bible Filter" speech*:

> *If you're trying to figure out the complexities of human behaviour, or your own behaviour and feelings, by running them through a Bible Filter, or by trying to conclude you're okay by the careful choice of words and phrases reflected in the*

> *Bible, and thereby ignoring your own behaviour. That you possess Free Will but are not exercising it, or that you ignore people's reactions to you and your behaviour and are not open to having a discussion on how to make your life better, which is the point of therapy, and you only want to prove that your belief system—the Bible—is the correct and only option, then you certainly don't need me.*

I believe it is right to set direction from one's beliefs and values. If you believe in God, then your values should reflect that belief, but—and this is my own belief—not to the point where you sacrifice your own *free will* and replace it with a dogmatic book of answers that incapacitates that free will.

A very spiritual friend of mine gave me a quote that summed it up for her: *"The Bible is filled with a lot of good stuff; some of it is even true."* She had lost her faith, but has never stopped looking for answers to life's problems from life itself. My client, however, found all his answers in a book and the reason for that choice became clearer as we talked.

Life had literally kicked the snot out of this person. His self-esteem was very low and hidden behind a continual outward show designed to convince everyone that he was "okay". But he was not okay! He had given up on people and decided to make "God" responsible for his life. "God's in charge, so I don't have to be", he shared in a session. "All I have to do is obediently follow His word and I will be fine." I asked about the belief that "God helps those who help themselves". He shrugged his shoulders and smirked that "I know the answer, but you don't" smile.

It was unfortunate that he sought refuge in a value system that had not really contributed to resolving his issues, which was, I inferred, the reason why he was in my office in the first place. I never bothered with the rest of my thoughts that might have provided him with a challenging new perspective—a perspective having to do with purpose in life, the need for balance, the ability to be aware of and control emotional states, meeting physical needs, resolving and overcoming intellectual challenges, and addressing spiritual needs.

I had shot my last bolt; I was spent. My best argument had been articulated in my "Bible Filter" speech. With his latest smirk still all over his face, I tried to sound intelligent, but could only come up with, "If we don't think and exercise our power of choice, we will end up ... with ... with ... a second round of Crusades!" We both started laughing so hard that for a moment we forgot just how far apart our belief systems were. The laugh was good, but I still got fired. He never came back.

There is rarely just one way to do something!
That goes for belief systems as well.

IN CONTROL

It is not always clear to me why people need to be *in control*? Is this a nature issue? Do humans just feel better, safer, and more confident when they are "in control?" Does it have something to do with the common perception that "if you don't agree with me—so often perceived as lack of control—then I feel rejected and I'll do anything not to feel the sting of rejection?" Or is it all of the above?

What I do know is that if a person plays "power games", they will be met with fear, resistance, resentment and sabotage. People will have to defend themselves against them. However, if people do not have to defend themselves, they are better listeners.

When talking about power, I differentiate between "going for control" and being "in charge" of one's self. When we *go for control*, our whole bearing is more aggressive, rigid in body and mind (thoughts). We become so focused on what we want to happen that we stop listening to others. If I can get you to think or do things my way, then I believe I am "in control", that I have power, that I am "the man" or "the woman", and I am worthy!

In contrast, being *in charge* is more of an assertive stance. We talk only for ourselves and do not need others to agree with us. We do not sell our point of view, but confidently express our own thoughts, feelings, values and beliefs using "I" language.[61]

We both have ways of thinking, seeing and doing things, we both have power, we are both important, and we are both worthy. I am "in charge" when I accept who you are and how you are different from me. And I am "in charge" when I share myself with you, confidently knowing "I am okay and you are okay."

So, if you want people to be less defensive and listen more to you when you speak, you will need to be less aggressive, less controlling, and more willing to share how you see things using "I" language.

> **We go for "control" of others
> when we are not "in charge" of ourselves.**

---

[61] Rosin, *Finding Balance*, p. 53.

DECISION MAKING

As humans, we really do try to do the best we can as often as we can! Nevertheless, some days we are irritable and impatient. Other days we are calm and able to think things through. Nobody *tries* to make a bad decision. We do the best we can at that moment. Period! Still, that isn't good enough for some people; they expect more from themselves.

He had to make a huge decision that affected the health of someone he really cared about. He agonized over the decision, and just when he had made up his mind, sabotaged the process with, "But what if ..." and plunged back into self-doubt. He turned all his options around to where none of them seemed "absolutely" correct—none are, but it didn't help to point that out—and ended up making no decision at all. He was frozen and needed Divine Intervention. Unfortunately, we were fresh out. I suggested:

> *Humans make "a" decision, not "the" decision. Only a Divine Being can do that. You are human. You will take the time to examine all the facts, and at some point you will just decide. You will make the best decision you can with the information you have, and you will live with it.*

Hindsight so often treats us harshly! When things don't work out as we had anticipated, it is easy to be hard on ourselves, particularly after we see the results of our decisions. It is important to remember that we make decisions every day, and to accept that we do the best we can with what we have at the time.

THE VALUE OF ACQUAINTANCES

If you want more friends in your life, stop looking for them! Making new friends can be a real problem. I often have the question posed to me during counselling: "How do I make new friends now that I am in my 50s?" I generally find that these clients have had the same difficulties in their 40s, 30s and 20s.

However, *why* this has been a problem throughout their life is not my focus. It is a fact that they have this difficulty, and that's that! What they can *do* to make new friends is the issue. But when they ask me *how* to make friends, I tell them sheepishly, "I am not really sure"—and I still charge the same fee!

What I do feel confident about, however, is that "the place to start making a friend is with the decision to stop looking to make one." It is said to be paradoxical when the *harder you try, the less you get!* This paradox factor will certainly interfere with the process of *making* someone a friend, so stop trying so hard and let it happen.

> *If you want a relationship to work, stop being so afraid to lose it, and laugh more.*

I think it is best to simply focus on an activity and have fun with the people—acquaintances—we meet at these activities. Stop being so serious, and stop making a concerted effort to make a lot of friends. I believe a person is very fortunate to have one or two really good friends in life. So stop at one or two friends and have several acquaintances. I believe you will have a lot more fun!

Remember, if you want to develop more relationships:

> *Choose activities that you enjoy and hook up with like-minded people who choose the same activities.*

Is the same true for interpersonal relationships? Can paradox be an issue? Can it be that the harder you try to make it work, the less likely it will work? I believe that to be true.

In my line of work, and based on what I have heard from the people I see, I would say that relationships are often a huge hassle in people's lives. Of course, people only come to see me when they have relationship problems, so I may be biased! However, in general, it seems to me that *acquaintances* make more sense and can be a lot of fun.

Despite what I say or what makes sense, the human animal will always keep trying to connect with others and make their special relationships work—sometimes at great personal cost. When we are in a relationship, change often occurs and sometimes we become needier. The lower the person's self esteem, the greater the fear of losing what they have in the relationship. We are desperate to make the relationship work. We become controlling. We are less relaxed and more serious and we end up having less fun. The experience provides almost the total opposite of what drew us into the relationship in the first place.[62][63][64]

---

[62] Rosin, *Finding Balance*, p. 32.
[63] Rosin, *Finding Balance*, p. 38.
[64] Rosin, *Finding Balance*, p. 67.

SAY "YES" TO YOURSELF

What makes you unique as a person is how you *Think, Feel, Value* and *Believe* (TFVB). These are your Principles.[65] So, why not share them? After all, they are who you are!

While most people know they have the right to express their principles, they choose not to express them. Who takes the time, or even has the time, to stop and define what their values are on a particular topic of discussion or what they actually believe? Sometimes, they are afraid of how they will be perceived. When people have little confidence, they generally choose to hide who they are—what they think, feel, value and believe—because they are afraid to be challenged on those principles.

To be able to say "yes" to yourself, you need to know who you are and what your principles are. You need to know what you stand for. And you need to have the freedom and self-confidence to express yourself, be able to say "yes" or "no" to others, and still be "okay" with yourself.

Unfortunately, "pleasure" is not a priority in many people's lives. Often what takes precedence is what other people think and their specific needs.

**Without a "Passionate Yes" and a "Courageous No",
you are not respected; you are used.**

---

[65] Rosin, *Finding Balance*, p. 53.

ABANDONMENT ISSUES

I have found that people are more disposed to letting go of old scars, hurts and resentments from the past if, as an adult, they find themselves in a *safe and loving relationship* where their needs are consistently met. However, because of the scars of low self-esteem, we often find that the partners we choose are incapable of providing that kind of safe and supportive environment.

One particular person, with whom I had been working for multiple sessions, began acting dramatically different. She wasn't saying much, but she was working very hard in her head. Finally she spoke, and the language of *abandonment* poured out.

The floodgates opened up about a childhood that was characterized by little to no support, put-downs and sexual abuse by a parent. I listened to her painful history, which had been brought to the surface again by the realization that her present relationship, which had languished for more than a decade, was in many ways similar to the relationship she had with her parent. Her present partner had few kind words for her, put her down, and was physically and emotionally unavailable to her. She thought these issues had been dealt with in previous therapy decades ago, but they had come back to haunt her present.

She had started the session with old feelings of abandonment and ended by identifying her current feelings of longing, emptiness and loneliness. She remained in a relationship with someone who could not possibly provide for her needs.

I attempted to interject some hope and pointed out:

> *"The difference between now and your youth was that in the past, as a child, you had no power to stop the abusive treatment. However, in the present, as an adult, you have power."*[66]

---

[66] Rosin, *Finding Balance*, p. 23.

Our job in therapy was to create a safe environment in which she could find the courage to push the boundaries and learn about her power.

It is sometimes difficult for abandoned and abused individuals to realize that they are different now. They are not defenceless and they have power. They must tap into that power in the present and the future if they are to have a different ending to their relationship stories than they have had in the past.

THE ADULT (A) OF A CHILD OF AN ALCOHOLIC

Much has been written on the subject of being the *child of an alcoholic* (COA). Hundreds of books and articles have sought to help those who have survived living with an alcoholic parent. A new thought occurred to me as I worked with a young man who had survived a very difficult childhood and adolescence, and was still "surviving" as an adult. As he told his story, I realized that ever since he was a child, he had taken responsibility for his alcoholic father. His father was basically a good guy, a happy drunk, and everybody's friend. My client had decided at an early age that the best way to deal with a father who was "never home, asleep at the bar at closing time, or his car was in the ditch" was to quietly look after things. He became the physical parent with strong adult (A) tendencies at a very young age.

It then struck me as interesting that COAs are *pressed into service early in life* and are forced to be *responsible* because of the chaos of living with an addicted parent who couldn't, or wouldn't—whatever you believe—take care of themselves, least of all to be a parent to their children.

All too often the coping mechanism necessary to survive such a youth is being overly responsible and it becomes a lifelong sentence with a unique set of symptoms that make it difficult to have healthy lives and relationships. It seems we need the opportunity to experience a healthy progression in regards to the various growth phases—infancy, childhood and adolescence— under the guidance of a caring and responsible adult(s). The COA skips being a child and, at an early age, goes directly to being an adult.

The *"child of an alcoholic"* is a phrase that one hears a great deal in the literature. However, even though it was the child that lost its youth when the young person got pressed into servicing the alcoholic parent, it was the adult (A)[67] of that child that "took charge" and made the decisions on how to survive in that family.

The days of our youth may be gone, but "It's never too late to have a happy childhood." Using the (A) for permission and the (FC) for creativity, let's design some real fun things to do in the present.

It seems that every alcoholic requires a responsible (A) to take care of them—even if that (A) belongs to a nine year old.

---

[67] Rosin, *Finding Balance,* p. 23.

WHAT A CHARACTER!

The importance of language was again confirmed for me while working with a client who had decided to isolate himself from people. He was firmly convinced that he had no people skills and would be better off if he just stopped socializing. He felt inclined to stay away from individuals and groups altogether. This became a recurring theme in our therapy. He confessed to me that he had been extremely blunt, consistently judgemental, and often impatient with many people over the years. These were not exactly the qualities that would endear him to the masses. However, as of late, he had improved. He told me that he was less intense, and a bit more laid back. I expressed that I also saw improvement, but he discounted my observation. "You *have to* see a difference. You're the therapist and that's what I pay you for."

I tried (with little success) to show him that he didn't have to "do everything perfectly". I didn't want him to think that he was worthy only when he went along with what others expected. I wanted him to understand that differences were okay, and that he was okay!

However, it wasn't until I reframed his behaviour by making the comment *you're a real character* that I struck a valid chord in him and was heard on this issue. I saw relief and resolve in his eyes. To me, his relief seemed to reflect the idea that "Perhaps my behaviour doesn't need to be totally changed—which is impossible, anyway. After all, if I 'cleaned up' too much, I wouldn't be a character, would I?"

For this client, there was some genuine happiness in being thought of by others as a *character*—being different. The resolution to his issues was in giving himself permission to be a character, and then understanding that being different from other people was okay and attributable to his being a "character", not because he was a defective person. Big, big smile!

We discovered some things that came to signify what being a positive "character" means. My take on it:

A character swims upstream, not to be different, but because that's the way they are going!

Characters are free, they have fun, know what they want, and don't need other people's permission to go and get what they want; they are free to take chances, to make a fool of themselves, to be honest, congruent and self-assured.

When "characters" speak out, they do it respectfully, using "I" language, with no blame in their voice. They accept how others see the world and are confident that they know what is best for themselves.

We agreed that differences between individuals are not only okay, but to be expected. That we humans are indeed very different! We have different gene patterns, different DNA, come from different backgrounds—culture, language, skin colour— amount of grey matter, and other differences. So being different isn't a bad thing; it's a natural thing.

Characters" are different, interesting, and very much okay!

THE CONTRACT

My client was feeling very emotional about his parents. He would burst into tears at the mere thought of their dying. He claimed that he needed them in order for him to continue living his life.

This prompted a discourse between the two of us that was focused on the difference between *wants* and *needs*. I described how want is a healthy and natural desire, while need is often a dysfunctional feeling that is attributable to a learned response. We had a lively follow-up discussion.

What I learned from that discussion is that I believe being born, living life and dying are quite natural. Not all that profound of a revelation I know, but wait, there's more! I also believe that there is an unspoken contract that each of us "signs" when we are born—you live and eventually you die. All proper and natural.

Now, you can sweat it and get in a flap about the final phase of the contract—that you, and others you love, will eventually pass away, for they, too, have signed a contract—or you can accept this final condition as a realistic part of life.

It is easy to treat this talk of the contract in a rather cavalier fashion, especially when one is not in imminent danger of dying. Dying too early or before we are ready, which is often true for most people, or dying of an illness that robs us of our dignity, has the ability to change one's perspective on this subject greatly. However, regardless of the hand we are dealt, it still plays out— we are born, we live, and we die.

So while we have the opportunity to appreciate, experience and enjoy the living phase of the contract, let's go all out! Let's live well and choose how we live! Let's stay in the moment and live life to the fullest! Appreciate the life that has been given and accept the end journey when the terms of our contract expire.[68]

**You are born
you live (and make sure it's to the fullest) you die!**

---

[68] Terry Jacks, *Seasons In The Sun,* Bell Records, Feb. 22, 1961.

WEIGHT FILTER

Angry and impatient, she was referred to me because of her negative outbursts. Not so surprisingly, the first thing out of her mouth was, "If I could only lose 60 pounds, I would be happy and not angry." She told me that for the past 35 years, she had been expressing a belief that she wouldn't be so angry if only she weighed less. But since nothing much had changed in that time, she was still heavy and still unhappy.

By linking her emotional well-being and happiness to the condition of weighing less, she had set herself on a path to perpetual disappointment. Her attempts to slim down weren't working, and even though she had lost considerable weight over the years, she had put it all back on. As a result, she was sick and tired of her life, and instead of celebrating her successes, and who she was, she allowed her setbacks to overcome her. The resulting cycle was wearing her down.

It became apparent to me that everything she did, at home or at work, was affected by her focusing on her belief about her weight. I called this focusing phenomenon her *Weight Filter*.

She knew immediately what I was getting at because she had already realized that most of her behaviours were in response to her obsession about her weight. Because she constantly thought about it, all decisions, judgements and interpretations, on a moment-to-moment basis, went through the *Weight Filter* before she responded or reacted.

The *Weight Filter* is much like a coffee filter where the water passes through the coffee and takes it to the cup. So, too, everything this woman thought, felt, valued and believed (TFVB) passed through her *Weight Filter* and was tainted by her feelings of being overweight, which, in turn, negatively influenced her feelings toward self and behaviours.

She gave me an example from earlier in the day when she was discussing a product with a customer. The whole time she was focusing on how the customer must be noticing the additional 30 lbs. she had recently put on. In her role as a salesperson, the *Weight Filter* led to a reduction of her professional abilities.

She understood that if she was to change and break free from the weight cycle she had been on most of her life, she would need to focus instead on what she wanted or needed to do—positive things. That would be the only way she could avoid sending everything through the Weight Filter, which was having a profoundly negative influence on her life.

She decided that she would give up the *Weight Filter* and substitute it with a *Wellness Filter*. Instead of aligning with negative feelings about her physical appearance, the *Wellness Filter* would keep her focused on healthy thoughts and behaviours.

Daily issues, problems, everything that she had previously related to her weight, and consequently always made her feel badly about herself, would now be traded for a completely new way of thinking—a focus on health and wellness and related activities and behaviours. The *Wellness Filter* would now encompass all aspects of her life (physical, social, etc.).

Whereas the *Weight Filter* is narrow, negative and deals with only one criterion—weight—the *Wellness Filter* is positive and enables a person to view themselves in a larger context according to their health and vitality.

Whereas the *Weight Filter* has people looking at life through a negative reinforcing lens, leaving them feeling bad about what they do and who they are, and that "the cup (life) is half empty", the *Wellness Filter* has people looking at life through a positive reinforcing lens, enabling them to focus on what is good in their lives and to see that "the cup is half full".

**Focus on your weight and feel like a failure,
or focus on wellness and feel like a winner.
Not such a difficult choice, eh?!**

INVITE PEOPLE TO THINK, NOT TO FIGHT!

The young man sitting across from me had a big ego and was sent to me because of his explosive temper. It was interesting to talk anger with this man because even though he was only half my age, I could easily identify with his aggressive responses.

As we shared with one another, we discovered that the one large difference between us was that I have more options in how I choose to respond to the *invitations* that others send me to get angry with them. We laughed when I stated, "Perhaps the biggest reason that I no longer react with anger has more to do with my age—my inability to duck or run as fast as I once did—than with good sense."

He told me that he believed he responds the way he does— with anger—because of an early childhood decision he had made. After a particularly bad beating from his father, he decided, "Nobody will ever push me around again." And from that point on, they hadn't. But as he grew older, he found that he no longer wanted to respond to his challenges with a physical response. Still, it was confusing for him. He didn't want to "be a wimp", but knew there had to be a better way to deal with differences than to use anger.

I introduced him to the *invitations concept*. Whenever he saw a personal challenge that he felt needed to be confronted—his first choice was to be angry—he now could reframe it as an invitation and either choose to respond or not to respond. He now had options. His dilemma, however, was that when he didn't respond to what he perceived to be the other person's challenge, he saw himself as less than a man.

My response was,

> "When you choose not to accept these invitations, you demonstrate that you are 'in charge' of yourself, that you are a responsible adult. This is the 'mark of a real man'. You can decide what is best for you—be 'proactive' and set your

own course in life, or just 'react' to others and let them be in charge of your life."

He understood, but at the same time, realised that he had been this way for a very long time. My having introduced him to a few new concepts would not suddenly change it all for him. He told me that he knew he needed to continue to reject what he now understood were *invitations* to get angry, to stay conscious of his rage, and to learn to exercise a great deal of self-discipline if he was to remain "in charge" of himself— as a real man—and make himself safe for others to be around.

He was not optimistic that he could change all at once, but he set up several sessions with me to continue his progress and seemed game to work at it. That was all I could ask. Where there's a will, there's a way!

Remember:
Invite people to think!
Talk to them, ask questions, investigate options,
share your own thoughts, feelings, values and beliefs
instead of demanding that they agree with you,
and don't bite on their invitation to respond with anger.

THERAPIST—MAGICIAN OR CHEERLEADER?

It's a Penn and Teller world of magic and illusion. On television, an illusionist made an entire Boeing 747 jet disappear, while another prestidigitator—yes, that is a word!—made the entire city of New York disappear before our very eyes. Sometimes things aren't really what they seem, and in the world of magic, it is the magician who is at the controls. In the world of therapy, the therapist is often thought to be in control and to possess the magic needed to bring about change. But I have certainly made the following point often enough in my writings—as therapists, we can't change others, we can only encourage people to change themselves!

Yes, we can be creative and lead people to experience new things, and yes, we can be a catalyst for change, but—and it's a big "but"— change will occur only if that person *chooses* to change.

Unfortunately, when an employer, a spouse or a court mandates that a person see a therapist, they often have the expectation that the therapist is "in charge" of that change—like a trickster who is able to pull a rabbit out of a hat. However, as I see it, the best a therapist can do is plant a seed, cheerlead, and then stroke the person mightily when they make good decisions.

We can't make people change.
We can only point out the benefits of their changing, and then be excited for them when they are successful.

WELLNESS, DESPITE THE EARLY MESSAGES

I have heard it said that between birth and six to eight years of age, we will have received the equivalent of 35,000 hours of taped messages. These messages are directives on how to live life, including the many *shoulds, have tos, got tos* and *musts*.

In this respect, it is important to realize that your family did what all good, bad or indifferent families do—their best. Some parents start out with a great deal more to offer their kids in terms of good, positive and mature messages, probably because they themselves were given more good as children by their parents. Some are more committed to being a parent and *getting it right* than others. But at heart, all parents want what is best for their children. Some notable exceptions are those parents who are mentally ill or abusive.

In general though, the messages that our parents or guardians passed on to us were meant to be helpful. And for the most part, they were.

However, what most parents—especially those born within one or two generations from the Great Depression—did not pass on to their kids were those skills and permissions needed to lead a *balanced life*. They often placed too much emphasis on work and paid too little attention to quality of life and personal well-being.

If Shakespeare had been thinking of my parent's generation, he might have penned, "Me thinks they know how to survive, but not necessarily how to be well!"

Walking a mile a day adds one year to your life!

LOVE BEGINS WITH RESPECT

When you "give in", "surrender" or say nothing about your needs or your T, F, V, B—thoughts, feelings, values and beliefs—you will often end up resentful and frustrated with yourself and your partner, or whomever, in whose presence you have chosen to remain silent. The "irrational belief" behind this silent behaviour quite often stems from a person's fears that "I will be rejected, taken to task or discounted if I am honest about what I think, feel, value and believe."

In some cases, you are correct; you will be criticized for your opinion. But more often than not, if you state what is on your mind, while you may not be particularly "liked" for holding that opinion, you will almost always be respected for sharing it. And you will certainly like yourself better.

The transition from "liking" to eventually "loving" another person is based on respect for that individual. It comes from the fact that they have had the courage to "state" who they are—for it does take courage to speak one's mind—and this sharing is perceived as *worthy of respect*.

Respect first, then love.

> **When you do speak up to share your thoughts, feelings, values and beliefs with others, do not imply (tone) that you have the "right" answer, only that your answer is right for you!**

REGRET!

My client had to make a major decision and could only see the realities of the situation in black or white—option 1 or 2. To help him overcome this dilemma, I introduced him to the concept of *Polarity Thinking*. He needed to take time to reflect and look for the shades of grey—other options – 3, 4, 5—that were available to him in between the *black and white*. This would give him the clarity he needed to make better quality decisions.

```
Black  !—————————!—————————!  White
1                  3,4,5                 2
```

In the diagram above, 1 and 2 represent opposites—the black and white, right or wrong, of any situation. When we are compelled to make a decision, these opposites are often the *knee-jerk* responses that present themselves to us in the moment and often do not work out for the best.

To break free from the narrow focus presented by decisions 1 and 2, it is important to take a moment to think and discuss our other options. It is equally important to be aware that it is our tendency to accept one of the polarities because it is easier to accept a knee-jerk reaction than to think things through. With knee jerk, the answer is just there. It is readily available and easily understandable in the face of the complexities of our particular situation.

When I illustrated the concept of polarity thinking, my client was already halfway toward finding an alternative option that was an appropriate fit for his particular circumstances. He had no difficulty in achieving and accepting a compromising middle position. In fact, he saw great value in this process.

In the course of our working together, we discovered that the usual factors that lead to polarity thinking were not the same for him. He was not particularly anxious about having to make decisions, or of making wrong ones, or moving too quickly.

No, his issue was imbedded in *regret*. He knew he had options, but feared that if he chose one over another, he might later regret his decision. He didn't want to "miss out on what the other options had to offer".

He carried the possibility of *regret* into his decision-making processes to the point where he was immobilized and really stuck. He ended up making no decisions at all, not because he couldn't see the options, but because he was afraid he would end up regretting the choice he did make. He wasn't getting anywhere fast!

Eventually he was able to identify and confront his feelings of regret. He became stuck less often by using the polarity thinking model to challenge himself to formulate options (3, 4, 5) and not just the immediate polar opposites (1, 2) where the extreme options were frightening to him. He learned to better accept and live with whatever decision was made, as long as it was well thought out.

STABILITY!

I find the issue of *control* very interesting. To be more precise, I am referring to control over our emotions, our actions and our lives. I think it amusing that we generally hate being controlled by others, and yet play all kinds of games to get the *upper hand* and be in *control* of them. Controlling and being controlled, either by laws or by common sense, are an integral part of life. One particular aspect of control that is often of great concern to each person is the issue of stability—steadiness, permanence—in our lives.

A number of my clients are on anti-depressant drugs. They take medication to stabilize their emotional highs and lows. But none of them likes the fact that they have to rely on a chemical in order to feel okay, to be in balance. They plan for the day when their medication can be reduced or eliminated. Until then, they are willing to live with the *forced stability* that these drugs provide. They feel it is a small price to pay for having both *the ability to think more rationally* and *an improved quality of life.*

I was discussing with a client about the pros and cons of taking his medication when he informed me that, shortly after beginning his latest regimen of a new drug, he no longer felt the highs or lows. Instead, he experienced a *mundane hum.* He felt *out of it,* which didn't sound good to me. So, I asked him to explain it to me on my mini blackboard:

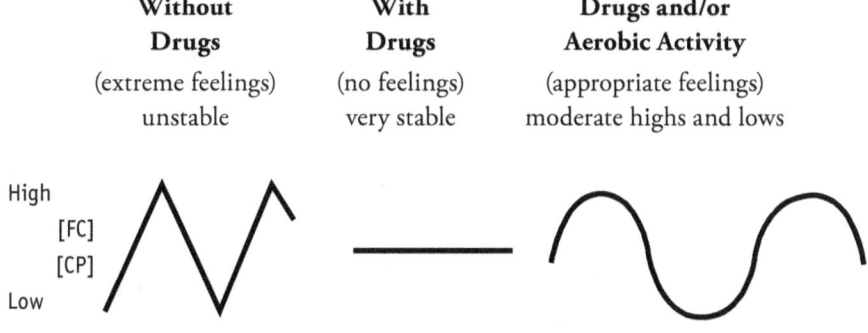

Having highs or lows that are out of control is not liveable. But being "too stable"—forced by drugs into having no highs or lows—is not desirable either. This is quite a dilemma for those taking medication.

It seems to me that when an individual's feelings move toward the *High* line (see diagram) they are probably responding to the impulses of their inner Fun Child[69] (FC)—they are in a positive place, able to enjoy themselves, able to be creative and optimistic. When they move toward the *Low* line, they are apt to become more judgemental, all knowing, with a strong Critical Parent[70] (CP) in charge of their lives.

Moving appropriately between highs and lows is the zone where a *stable* life is lived. Any extreme, including situations where the individual is never stable or always stable, is simply not desirable.

Life would be too boring and predictable, too automatic, lifeless, if our feelings were always the same. With or without chemical help, normal life should be in a constant state of flux, moving between the moderate highs and lows, not just stuck in neutral.

I believe Hans Selye was referring to such a condition when he implied that we need *variety and spice* in our life to be healthy.[71]

My client and I agreed with Selye.

**The only thing stable in human life
is the fact that we will always be subject to instability!**

---

[69] Eric Berne, *Games People Play*, New York, NY, Grove Press, 1964, p. 25.
[70] Eric Berne, *Games People Play*, p. 25.
[71] Hans Selye, *Stress Without Distress*, New York, NY, Signet, 1974, p. 83.

SIGNIFICANT MOMENTS

"We don't have time for us anymore!"
"We are too busy—work, kids, the house, we just survive."

This is what I often hear when I suggest to couples that they need to set aside more time for each other. I suggest that they not only *do* "stuff" together, like fun and relaxing activities, but they have enough energy at the end of the work day to truly enjoy activities so it doesn't feel like more work.

Time is a very precious commodity in today's frantic lifestyle. But if relationships are to thrive and not just survive—many aren't even doing that—then we need to make time for each other. Because of the lack of time for togetherness, I suggest to my clients that they use what time they do have together more efficiently.

You may have only a short period of time to spend with your partner before you gulp down supper and rush to get one kid to ballet and the other to soccer. But I ask them to think of the impact it would have on their relationship if they used even these short periods of time to *share and show concern* to each other. To look them in the eyes, maybe touch their shoulder, stand close to them, and create a *significant moment* in the middle of a busy time.

If your life is—or if you have allowed your life to be—a whirlwind of activities, then you need to ensure that your relationship is filled with many significant moments. Your partner needs to experience that you truly care about them. And when you stop in the middle of a whirl-wind in order to create a small significant moment, you do give a clear message to that person that you care about them.

There are times when presents, flowers and trips are appropriate, but between those times we need many intense *Active Listening*[72] sessions with

---

[72] Rosin, *Finding Balance*, p. 47.

our partner, lots of touching and demonstrations of caring— *significant moments*.

We need many of these short moments to get and keep a relationship healthy. Your partner needs to experience you reaching out to them, to know that you truly care about them, and when you stop in the middle of a whirlwind—your life—and create a *significant moment*, you give them a clear message of caring.

> *Doing things for others when it is inconvenient for you will get you many more strokes than when it is easy for you! It will be seen as a sacrifice and will have a higher stroke value.*

**Two minutes well spent can save a life—
the life of a relationship.**

THE FOURTH PRIMARY INFLUENCER

Perhaps this is just another heading where I can store more "stuff" that I can't otherwise find a place for. Or perhaps I have found one of the great secrets of the "Human Condition"— whatever that is! I am speaking about what I call the *Fourth Primary Influencer*.

The first three Primary Influencers are *Heredity, Environment,* and what I call (individual) *Character*. The first two are often cited in literature as helping to describe why people "feel and act" the way they do. The Fourth Influencer, as proposed by moi, may not be as steeped in supportive research as the first two, but it is significant in explaining why "good people do bad things".

I have been asked many times by individuals in obvious remorse, "Why do I yell at my wife in public? Why do I commit adultery, give the finger in traffic, cheat a store clerk, stay angry at a parent for something that happened years ago, or be a jerk to my kids?" Good people doing inappropriately bad things. Why? Stop asking why and stop doing the bad things. But if you absolutely have to know why, pay attention.

I think the Fourth Primary Influencer could perhaps answer the "Why of all Why" questions, assuming you're prone to asking "why" questions, which I am not.[73] If, however, it turns out to be less than significant, then this Fourth Primary Influencer will just be a place to "file" all the questions, reasons and behaviours that don't fit into the other three Influencer categories.

The Fourth Primary Influencer is—and hold on to your hats for this one! Drum roll please!—*being human! Humanness*! Tada!!

After living many years on this planet, I have come to believe that the Supreme Being, whomever or whatever your belief on this issue is, humans got made "less than perfect" and that was by design. The human species is incredibly complex, interestingly unpredictable, and incredibly flawed.

---

[73] Rosin, *Communication & Relationships*, p. 157.

Being imperfect is what makes us "humanlike" instead of "God-like" and keeps life more interesting!

However, being human is not intended to be an excuse or a way out of taking responsibility for inappropriate behaviour. Instead, this definition is to be used to understand the unexplainable behaviours of good people who make serious mistakes.

Now there is no need to ask "why" questions ever again!

TIME TOGETHER ISN'T THE WHOLE ANSWER, BUT ...

It was my first session with this couple. He had seen me once before on his own, and had described how unhappy he was. As a consequence of this bad relationship, he had even begun "leering at women in the work-place!"

This session was quite informal and they chatted about how their relationship had changed over the years to the point where it was now one "of convenience". His analysis was, "She doesn't care much about sex and I have stopped pushing for it."

The hour went by quickly and I suggested that we meet again to explore what they both wanted to do about the *empty place* they had fallen into.

Our second session took place on a snowy Saturday at a time when, as he declared, he "usually had a nap!" I wasn't sure what to make of this declaration. She was her usual, timid self, but I detected a resolve and strength that said he was not going to get out of this relationship so easily.

It was obvious to me that he was trying to force her to do all the work and make all the changes in order to save their relationship. I suggested that his lack of involvement, which carried over into counselling, was "a great way to sabotage the process and guarantee that it will fail".

We discussed how their backgrounds contributed to their present situation. We examined how they met, their first couple of years together, family life, lifestyle choices, and, inevitably, how their sex life had changed to where he now felt "nothing sexual for her".

Before they departed at the end of the session, I encouraged them to agree to spend some time together and engage in more fun activities. And I included the edict that they have "absolutely no sex"—as if they would at that point anyway!

It wasn't exactly the most dramatic therapeutic intervention I could offer, but one that I felt necessary. At least they would be in the same room doing something together. No swords were drawn and they were even smiling a little. Lots of work lay ahead for this couple, but they had at least given themselves permission to start.

I'm not sure why, but sometime between our second and third sessions, I began to reflect on the work of noted Jewish physiotherapist *Dr. Feldenkrais*. Stay with me—it has relevance! Dr. Feldenkrais had pioneered a particular method of body work, and as I understood it, when primary muscle and nerve pathways are damaged, it becomes possible, through manipulation, to create new pathways around the injury and restore function.

Feldenkrais demonstrated that when original nerves and muscles responsible for a certain movement can no longer function due to injury or disease, it was possible to restore movement by working around the injury with secondary nerves and muscles, helping to focus the mind on rerouting messages to a substitute muscle. He believed that our memory stores cues, and that it is difficult to prevent associated feelings from flooding back when those cues are presented.

My male client had developed a few negative cues from previous experiences in the bedroom. His perception was that he had been sexually rejected many times. Immediately upon entering the bedroom, he would turn cold and construct a "wall". I referred to it as the *frozen chasm*, and they agreed that they could actually feel the coolness between them in the bedroom. So something needed to be done about the bedroom cues. What popped into my mind was not Brief Therapy[74] or Cognitive Restructuring,[75] two common techniques used in these situations, but Feldenkrais.[76] Go figure!

On the surface, this is all very nice—Feldenkrais rerouting nerves, restoring muscle function using various cues, etc. But what did this have to do with my clients' problems in the bedroom? Maybe nothing, but the

---

[74] Fisch, Weakland, Segal, *The Tactic of Change*, San Francisco, CA, Jossey-Bass, Inc., 1982.
[75] Elizabeth Scott, M.S., *Cognitive Restructuring for Stress Relief*, about.com, Nov. 29, 2007.
[76] Yochanan Rywerant, *The Feldenkrais Method*, San Francisco, CA, Harper & Row, 1983.

whole issue of cues and how they can set us up positively or negatively before anything is even said or done, got me thinking that this was perhaps truest for the male partner in this relationship.

Based on past negative experience, he no longer sent messages from his brain to his libido when he entered the conjugal bed. Although he confided that he felt nothing for her, my assessment of the situation was that it was actually worse than nothing. In fact, he felt anger, disappointment, and the need to snipe at her. The kind of cues he was seeing and feeling were not the kind that would ever lead to his feeling frisky toward his partner.

Methinks we need to replace his old, negatively imprinted cues with new, positive ones!

When I posed this rather bizarre and elongated theory as a potential solution to their problem, they shrugged and looked at each other with a kind of, "He took all this time just to tell us this?" Then he interrupted their puzzled stares by interjecting, "You mean, I need to do something different, so that my brain will perceive the bedroom and my wife differently, positively, so that I will feel friskier?"

Bingo! Here I was, afraid that they might not get the message, and he synthesized it in a nutshell! Shame on me for not having more faith in people! She chuckled, "You need to send more messages to that part of your anatomy—you know, the part that men think with! "We all laughed, and both he and I concurred with her analysis.

The couple agreed to develop a new set of cues for the bedroom, and as starters they proposed engaging in fun activities with each other (i.e., cards, chess), purposeful discussions, sharing popcorn, back massages, and reading to one another. And off they went with my stern warning—"no sex, it's too early! Remember we just want to warm up the bedroom, not start a fire."

It turned out that it didn't take long for him to re-wire his brain and for them to ignore my stern warning of no sex. Some people just don't listen to sound counsel. Go figure!

Remember, when you:

Change the cues, you change the feelings.
When you change the feelings, you change the behaviour.
Frisky is good!

DEFINING MOMENT

A *defining moment* is an understanding, an epiphany, and clarity of mind that a person arrives at in life. It is one of those moments that provide a compass—a direction for all that comes after that moment so that one is confident in the direction they will go. This moment sets the tone for our feelings and behaviour. This guidepost will often remain in place until ... well ... until you have another defining moment!

There is a defining moment when we decide to love a person, to live together, to get married, to get divorced, or when the partner finds out about "the affair".

The defining moment that results from an affair sets into motion several feelings that can lead to a severe lack of trust between partners. The offended partner often feels hurt, humiliated and betrayed by the other's actions.

This "moment" is the lens that people use to judge the relationship thereafter, and then to treat their partner accordingly. Unless the wounded partner can experience another defining moment—one that will have more positive results—there is little hope for the restoration of trust.

After the affair, couples come into counselling feeling hurt, betrayed, angry and embarrassed. Many truly desire to get over the bad feelings and return to being a family again. However, there is a "but", and that is very often because the betrayed person doesn't easily let go of their feelings of betrayal.

Traditionally, I have found that when the male partner has the affair, he is exceptionally sorry and really "aims to please" his partner in the first few weeks after the discovery. Soon, though, he tires of the "remorseful" position that he feels obliged to assume and comes to resent his partner's leverage in the relationship.

He begins to stop "walking on eggshells", starts becoming angry more often—like before the affair—and starts expressing feelings of frustration, like, "Let it go, that's in the past" or "It's over, she means nothing to me."

He expects his partner to simply shut off her feelings— which would certainly meet his needs—and to "get on with life".

On her part, the resumption of his anger and frustration really scare her because "the relationship is starting to feel just like it did before the affair".

It was a dreary, rainy morning and we were three quarters through our second session of rehashing the affair and all its sordid details. This couple had been doing a lot of talking between the sessions—admittedly "some of the best we have ever done". However, in spite of these good talks, she couldn't dismiss her feelings of betrayal.

The defining moment in their relationship was cemented—hurt, anger, betrayal—several weeks previously when she learned of his infidelity. Nothing was going to alter her perception in the present or future; and she would continue to direct her feelings—hurt, anger, betrayal—and resultant behaviours toward him, unless she could create a new defining moment—one built on hope and trust.

She had come to counselling to receive help in overcoming these destructive feelings. On his part, he attended the sessions because he was fed up with having the affair thrown in his face, especially when he was "trying so hard and being so understanding".

I asked both of them if they thought it was possible to create a *new defining moment*. Or, did they just have to wait for time to heal all wounds? Could they create it before they both lost hope and he lost his temper? I asked her what she needed to do to let go of her anger. "Do you need to berate him verbally? Do you need to write to him and put all your feelings down on paper? Do you need to look him in the eye and ask him questions such as, 'Are you back to stay or only until next time?', 'Can I trust and depend on you?', and 'Are you willing to work on our relationship to make it better?' (better, but not back to normal)."

And yes, I did state, "Look him in the eye and decide if he is telling the truth."*

---

* I can just hear some of you saying, "How naïve! Don't you know he could lie and deceive her and you'd be helping him to set her up to be hurt again?" I do believe people make mistakes and need second chances. If he is foolish enough to reject what you have to offer a second time, you will know and you will act appropriately by hiring an absolute barracuda for a lawyer. But until you "know", act lovingly.

I knew that if she could decide whether he was being truthful through such an encounter, then that could be the new defining moment they needed. They could then decide to move ahead and work on recreating their broken relationship.

TWO STREAMS OF LEARNING

I believe there are *two major streams* of learning from which the majority of the messages that direct our lives come.

One stream begins when we are born and continues through until we become an adult. A second stream begins after adolescence and when we move into our "professional" life.

It is said that we accumulate in our brain somewhere in the neighbourhood of *20,000–25,000 hours of tape* on how we should, have to, and must do life by the time we are 12 years old. Add a few more experiences and inputs from significant people in our lives, (parents, siblings, friends, church, community, teachers, coaches—you get the idea), and by the time we are through our post-secondary education or out in our first job, we have probably added another 5,000–10,000 more messages about how we should do life. This is the *first stream* of learning that moulds us into whom we become, the essence of our personhood.

The *second stream* begins after we graduate high school, complete university or post-secondary education, or enter the real work world. We begin to flex our professional muscles and gain confidence in ourselves. That is why a person can be very confident and assertive in their job as a teacher or welder (*second stream*) and yet so passive in their interpersonal relationships (*first stream*).

I believe our adult behaviours come from these different learning streams! One stream (interpersonal) much baggage and many "shoulds" that have been accumulating since birth. The other stream begins when we start our academic job training as a young adult and this stream is not encumbered by emotional life lessons but rather by what is learned through academic and professional training.

It is very possible to be highly proficient in one's "Professional" life, yet very dysfunctional in their "Interpersonal" life.

Also by Dan Rosin:

For more than five decades I have worked with clients in counselling/therapy to help them solve there 'living' issues. As well, I have penned many articles on the subject and have conducted numerous workshops, speaking to thousands of people on the effects of stress, the promotion of wellness, the development of in-house prevention teams – all to encourage people to take better care of themselves.

Time in counselling/therapy has often been reduced by an on-target concept, such as those that fill the pages of this book. These concepts help 'cut to the chase' and invite understanding and insight with a minimum of verbiage.

Finding Balance is a collection of insights, concepts, and stories designed to help readers develop healthier attitudes toward work, relationships, and the achievement of well-being. It is informed by research and inspired by many years of counselling and therapeutic practice, and hundreds of hours as a workshop facilitator. The concepts are derived from composites of many different sessions with many different clients.

My hope with the republishing of *Finding Balance* was to reach a new generation of Manitobans as well as new readers across Canada and the United States. Our lives are becoming increasingly complex and busy and I think the book is as relevant today as when I first published it. Sales are presently over 10,500 copies.

I believe people are reading this book for the following reasons:

- To better understand the stressors in their lives, their driven behaviour, and how best to be 'in charge' of their lives,
- To discover more about self and in particular, why they don't take better care of self,

- To alter their perspective so they can see 'change' as a positive thing instead of something to be avoided, and
- To achieve their objectives and become healthier, happier, and lead more balanced lives.

Finding Balance can be purchased at theewingspublishing.com, Google, Amazon, Barnes & Noble.

www.ingramcontent.com/pod-product-compliance
Lightning Source LLC
LaVergne TN
LVHW041804060526
838201LV00046B/1114